COMMUNICATION IN THE CLASSROOM

Original Contributions by

Larry L. Barker, *Auburn University*

Donald J. Cegala, *Ohio State University*

D. Thomas Porter, *Purdue University*

Gustav W. Friedrich, *University of Oklahoma*

William R. Todd-Mancillas, *Rutgers University*

Peter Andersen, *San Diego State University*

Janis Andersen, *San Diego State University*

Vicki S. Freimuth, *University of Maryland*

Jean M. Civikly, *University of New Mexico*

COMMUNICATION IN THE CLASSROOM
Original Essays

Edited by
Larry L. Barker
Auburn University

Prentice-Hall, Inc., Englewood Cliffs, New Jersey 07632

Library of Congress Cataloging in Publication Data
Main entry under title:

Communication in the classroom:

    Includes bibliographies and index.

    Contents: An introduction to classroom com-
munication / Larry L. Barker—The role and
assessment of prerequisite behaviors in communication instruction / Donald J. Cegala—Theoretical
explorations / Thomas Porter—[etc.]

    1. Interaction analysis in education—Addresses,
essays, lectures. 2. Oral communication—Addresses,
essays, lectures. 3. Teacher-student relationships
—Addresses, essays, lectures. 4. Classroom
management—Addresses, essays, lectures.
I. Barker, Larry Lee, date.
LB1033.C63   371.1'022   81-13951
ISBN 0-13-153551-X   AACR2

Editorial/production supervision and interior design by Kate Kelly
Manufacturing buyer: Edmund W. Leone

Printed in the United States of America

10 9 8 7 6 5 4 3 2 1

ISBN 0-13-153551-X

Prentice-Hall International, Inc., *London*
Prentice-Hall of Australia Pty. Limited, *Sydney*
Prentice-Hall of Canada, Ltd., *Toronto*
Prentice-Hall of India Private Limited, *New Delhi*
Prentice-Hall of Japan, Inc., *Tokyo*
Prentice-Hall of Southeast Asia Pte. Ltd., *Singapore*
Whitehall Books Limited, *Wellington, New Zealand*

This Manuscript Is Dedicated to the Memory of

ROBERT J. KIBLER

CONTENTS

CHAPTER FOUR
CLASSROOM INTERACTION   55
Gustav W. Friedrich

CHAPTER FIVE
CLASSROOM ENVIRONMENTS
AND NONVERBAL BEHAVIOR   77
William R. Todd-Mancillas

CHAPTER SIX
NONVERBAL IMMEDIACY IN INSTRUCTION   98
Peter Andersen and Janis Andersen

CHAPTER SEVEN
COMMUNICATION APPREHENSION
IN THE CLASSROOM   121
Vicki S. Freimuth

CHAPTER EIGHT
SELF-CONCEPT, SIGNIFICANT OTHERS, AND CLASSROOM COMMUNICATION

146

Jean M. Civikly

FOREWORD

Gerald R. Miller

The papers in this volume speak to a number of crucial issues concerning classroom communication. Though their thrust is cognitive, their genesis is affective—each is a labor of love dedicated to a trusted teacher and a valued colleague, Robert J. Kibler.

I believe Bob Kibler would have praised these papers. Of course, he would have tempered his praise with cogent, constructive criticism; for Bob always assumed that everyone's work, including his own, could profit from currying and polishing. What he would have applauded is their collective emphasis on vital aspects of the classroom communication process, as well as the efforts of each author to illumine his or her area conceptually and empirically.

It is worth recalling the tremendous contribution Kibler himself made to kindling systematic empirical study of instructional development and classroom communication. When I was pursuing my Ph.D. in the late fifties, very little of the work in what was then called "speech education" was of an empirical bent—at least, not in the sense that scholars in the area sought to arrive at stochastic generalizations about factors influencing the development of competent communicators or variables impinging upon the effectiveness of classroom communication instruction. Efforts to identify the characteristics of good teaching typically centered on case studies or vignettes of redoubtable teachers of the past, while instructional objectives were usually cloaked in verbally elegant, yet behaviorally ambiguous language. If they existed at all, conceptual schemes and programmatic research strategies for improving the overall quality of communication instruction were certainly in their infancy.

Bob Kibler, along with several of the authors appearing in these pages, was largely responsible for remedying this shortcoming. Due to his efforts and those of his colleagues, Larry Barker and William Brooks, Purdue University gained a reputation as *the* center of excellence for the behavioral study of communication education in the early sixties—a reputation sustained by the later contributions of scholars such as Gustav Friedrich. When the "Barker and Kibler Show" (as it was sometimes humorously, but always respectfully, referred to by certain members of the field) moved south to Florida State University, its creativity and energy remained vigorously intact. During the late sixties and early seventies, Kibler and his students completed several seminal projects, among the most noteworthy being the work on behavioral objectives referred to by Cegala in this volume.

Despite his many scholarly commitments, Kibler made the time to participate extensively in both the International Communication Association and the Speech Communication Association. In 1968, Barker and he performed a major service for the field by agreeing to take on the time-consuming, thankless task of editing *Conceptual Frontiers in Speech-Communication,* the report of the SCA New Orleans Conference on Research and Instructional Development. In 1976–77, in his role as president-elect of ICA, Kibler planned the first annual meeting of that association held outside the continental confines of North America—the highly successful conference in West Berlin. And in 1977–78, he not only gave unselfishly of his time and energy as president of ICA, he climaxed the year with a memorable party at the Chicago conference for *all* the association's members. Those who knew Bob realize that the only way he could host a presidential party was by adopting an open-door policy, for while he recognized the administrative necessity of an association "power structure," he was at heart a proponent of democracy in our professional societies.

Although I have left many things unsaid about Bob Kibler's professional and personal gifts to his field, the papers in this volume, authored by his students, colleagues, and friends, speak more eloquently to those gifts than I could ever do. Following his untimely death, the eulogies by some of his admirers took on a hyperbolic air that, while understandable, would probably have perplexed Bob. Like the rest of us, he had his quirks and idiosyncrasies, and at times he fell short of the demanding goals he set for himself. Through it all, however, the two characteristics I recall most vividly were his cautious optimism about the field and his uncompromising honesty—Bob Kibler is the only editorial board member I can recall during my editorship of *Human Communication Research* who always began a tardy review by exonerating the editor and emphasizing that complaints about the tardiness should be laid at his doorstep. My reading of the papers in this volume reveals the same two qualities: optimism about the progress that has occurred in our understanding about classroom communication, and honesty about the many problems that remain unsolved. I suspect Bob Kibler would have endorsed heartily such a legacy to our field.

PREFACE

The decade of the 1980s promises to be both exciting and rewarding for the discipline of Communication Education. The individual disciplines of Education and Communication have overlapped and intertwined for several decades. However, it appears that, for the first time, scholars are recognizing the interdependence between the two cognate areas. This recognition has spawned new research and theory in the ecclectic discipline of Communication Education. This volume is dedicated to this new discipline and the accompanying cooperative efforts of its teachers. In particular, this volume is dedicated to the late Dr. Robert J. Kibler, who foresaw this trend several years ago, and helped train a generation of scholars to further the discipline.

This volume is designed to serve as a textbook in courses dedicated to Communication Education, Communication Instruction and Communication for the Classroom Teacher. All of the authors are experts in Communication Education, and all were directly touched by the life of Robert J. Kibler, either as colleagues or students.

It is the intent of those of us involved with this project to provide a text that is not only filled with "hard" data, but which is also teachable. Our thanks to many students and colleagues who worked hard to help the book come to fruition. Particular thanks goes to Drs. Robert Cox, Frederick Williams, and

Gerald Miller of the International Communication Association who encouraged us to undertake the project. Thanks also goes to Ed Stanford and the Editorial Staff of Prentice-Hall who helped make the project a reality, and to Sharon Kibler for her special contributions.

This book not only stands as a memorial to Bob Kibler, but all royalties are being donated by Authors and Contributors to the ICA's Robert J. Kibler Memorial Fund.

Larry L. Barker
Auburn University

CHAPTER ONE
AN INTRODUCTION TO CLASSROOM COMMUNICATION

Larry L. Barker*

*Dr. Barker is Alumni Professor, Department of Speech Communication, at Auburn University, Auburn, Alabama.

THE DYNAMICS
OF COMMUNICATION
IN THE CLASSROOM

The communicative act must be studied in context. In this chapter the emphasis is on communication as it occurs in the classroom. The components and processes of classroom communication are similar to those in other settings, but the functions and patterns of classroom communication are unique. An illustration may help make these relationships and differences more apparent. In business and industry, civic organizations, service fraternities, religious institutions, and similar groups communication plays a vital role in informing and/or persuading group members. Information sharing among individuals is seldom the primary goal of such groups. Decisions which are made through communication in these organizations generally affect the goals, activities, or success of the group rather than the individual member. Persuasion is often the primary goal of communication among group members, and the objective of providing information is often secondary.

In the classroom, communication is also important. However, in this setting *information sharing* among teacher and students is the primary goal. Intrapersonal, interpersonal, group, and cultural communication provide vehicles for the transmission of information in the classroom. Thus, the maximum impact of communication is on the *individual,* not a larger corporate body or organization. When persuasion occurs in the classroom, it is often as a result of increased understanding brought about through informative communication. Impact of communication upon participants is more lasting in the classroom than in most other group communication settings because of the interpersonal nature of classroom communication between student and teacher.

In the preceding comparison, processes and components in each communication context were similar. However, purposes and message impact were significantly different. Few observers would deny that classroom communication is one of the most important communication forms occurring in society. The oral interaction which occurs in the classroom affects the personality development, intellectual development, and social development of students and teachers alike.

The differences in communication context are not only a function of the differences in environment and geographical setting, but are also a function of the way in which observers and participants perceive the context. For example, teachers are perceived differently in the United States than teachers in European and Asian countries by their respective citizens. In India, for example, the teacher enjoys one of the highest positions of respect in the nation. In America the teacher holds a somewhat less prestigious position, although he or she is regarded in general as trustworthy, honest, patriotic, dedicated, and often "poor." It is obvious that all teachers in India are probably not deserving of high respect, nor are all teachers in America necessarily poor or patriotic. The point is that in a communication setting the perception of the context by both observers and participants tends to alter the outcomes of the communication experience.

Conversely, teachers often unjustly categorize certain types of students in the classroom on the basis of race, creed, color, or their family name. This perception can negatively affect the teachers' reaction to the child and interfere with successful teacher-student communication.

Included in the process of perceiving the situation is the conception of one's role in the situation. Children who have been enculturated to view education as a waste of time and a "sissy" process will probably perceive themselves differently in the classroom setting than students who have been taught that education is both necessary and socially desirable. A study conducted at the University of Chicago Urban Child Center supports this point. The investigation demonstrated that mothers of lower-class black children tend to define their child's role in the classroom as one of passive acceptance. Middle-class black mothers generally define their child's role in a more active context which stimulates greater participation in the educational process (Shipman & Hess, 1966). Such social influences also affect childrens' perceptions of their teacher and his or her role in the classroom.

The written and unwritten rules of the communication context can also affect communication outcomes. In the classroom the "rules" are largely determined by social conventions and customs, school board policies, local administrator preferences, and teacher preferences. The degree to which the rules are implicit or explicit will also affect their impact upon the setting.

THE COMMUNICATION PROCESS

Within the various levels of communication there are certain basic components and processes which do not change. Each of these components and processes may be composed of several subparts and perform a variety of functions. The following diagram demonstrates the directional flow and relationships among the components in the communication cycle.

Originator

In classroom communication the teacher is frequently the originator of the message. In one investigation of teacher verbal behavior it was discovered that, depending on the degree of teacher dominance, teachers initiated from 55.2% to

80.7% of all messages in the classroom (Jackson 1965). The communication "cycle" is usually initiated as a result of the originator-teacher's need to impart information or the student-originator's need to seek information. The need to communicate may also result from a stimulus (or stimuli) which affects the originator. These stimuli may evolve from within the originator, such as hunger or thirst, a headache, or a sudden "flash" of an idea. Stimuli are also supplied by the immediate environment. Books, pictures, questions from other persons, and physical action all stimulate the communicative act in the classroom.

The originator is more than a speaker because he or she utilizes both verbal and nonverbal channels. He or she can communicate ideas through gestures,

FIGURE 1-1   The Communication Process

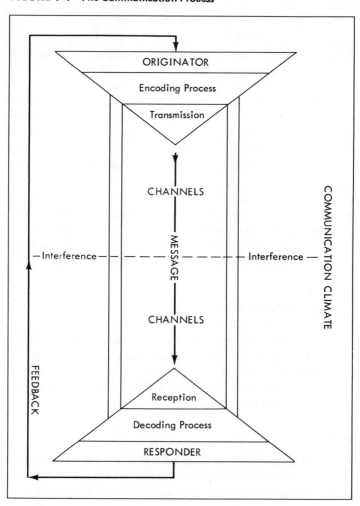

bodily action, facial expression, and physical appearance, as well as through words and pictures. The source of the message is usually the brain or central nervous system (CNS). The originator (either teacher or student), consciously or subconsciously conceptualizes an idea which needs to be expressed and then transmits it. He or she transmits a message in order to induce a reaction from the responder. If he or she fails to achieve a response, the need to communicate is not satisfied, and the communication "cycle" is broken.

Encoding

The encoding process transforms thoughts and ideas into word symbols, bodily movements, facial expression, and/or gestures. It involves both conditioned responses (natural reflexes) and cognitive responses which require varying degress of mental deliberation. On both cognitive and conditioned response levels the encoding process interacts with the originator's individual communication climate. Such elements in the climate as hereditary influence, past experience, and social development tend to mold the originator's encoding system into a particular pattern. The originator must also be aware of the responder's communication climate and related encoding system in order that the encoded symbols will be understood by the responder.

Transmission

Transmission involves the sending of coded messages through a specific channel or channels. These channels are usually light waves and sound waves in human communication. In human verbal communication the transmitter may be thought of as a complex of bodily components which actually produce the sounds of speech. In nonverbal, physical communication the transmitters are intricate systems of smooth muscles and nerves which generate and control bodily movement and facial expression.

Message

In classroom communication the message is actually a spatial extention of the originator. It carries meaning to a responder across space and/or time and allows him or her to achieve a response or satisfy a communication need with minimal physical effort. Messages may be categorized according to their desired impact upon the responder. Such a classification would include primary messages, secondary messages, and unintentional messages. The *primary messages* convey the most important ideas in the channel which the originator selects as most effective for the particular message. In most classroom communication this channel is the aural channel. Secondary messages also convey important ideas but tend to reinforce or amplify meaning conveyed in the primary message. Examples of secondary messages include a nod of the head accompanying an affirmative answer to a question, or a gesture of the hand accompanying a set of directions.

The channel in these instances is visual. Unintentional messages are transmitted constantly by the originator but bear little relationship to the primary and secondary messages which carry the intended meaning. They can, however, detract from these more important messages if they produce negative reactions in the responder. Such physical features as careless dress, uncontrolled or habitual gestures, absent-minded pacing, or unkempt appearance can transmit negative unintentional messages to the responder. Unintentional messages cannot completely be eliminated, but they can be controlled so that their effect becomes neutral or positive.

Channels

Channels are the pathways upon which the messages travel. In intrapersonal (within the individual) communication these are neural pathways and smooth muscles. In interpersonal, group, and cultural communication the channels are frequently light waves and sound waves which carry visual and spoken messages to be received and decoded by the responder.

Communication Climate

The communication climate is the sum total of the originator's and responder's past and present hereditary, social, and personal influences which have affected their personality, language, and physical development. As a general rule, when the communication climate of the originator and responder is similar, the communication will be more effective and fewer breakdowns and misunderstandings will occur. In an ideal setting the communication climate of originator and responder is identical. In reality this condition rarely if ever exists. Even between identical twins communication climates differ because of such factors as parental attention, social contacts, and exposures to different language settings.

Interference

In most communication settings noise or interference is present which can alter the message. Such interference may be both internal and external to the originator or responder. Internal interference may take such forms as physical pain or tiredness. This physiological interference tends to alter or disturb normal communication processes and to make encoding and message formation processes less efficient. External interference may occur in one of two forms, either aural or visual. Aural interference in the classroom setting may take the form of whispering, sounds in the hall, sounds of passing automobiles, or a variety of external audible distractions. Visual interference in the form of unerased writing on the blackboard behind the teacher, moving objects which may be seen out the window, or unfavorable lighting conditions may detract from the originator's message. All forms of interference may be reduced through conscious effort, but it is virtually impossible to eliminate them completely. When the teacher understands that interference tends to alter messages and may act as a barrier to effective communication, he or she may take appropriate steps to reduce its negative effects.

Reception

At a given instant, countless stimuli bombard the originator from his or her immediate environment. Some of these are strong enough to be perceived at the conscious level, while others are so weak they are not even noticed. The process by which these stimuli are received is termed reception. The bodily receptors include the eyes, nose, ears, tongue, and skin, as well as sensory receptors beneath the skin which perceive heat and pain. In speech communication the primary receptor is the eardrum. In intrapersonal communication receptors are sensory proprioceptive organs which interact with the brain and the cental nervous system. It is important to note that although many stimuli are received, only those which are interpreted by the brain affect behavior. It is theoretically possible to react to all stimuli we receive but, in practice, we usually are not sufficiently sensitive to perceive all stimuli which might potentially stimulate communication.

Decoding

The decoding process is the reverse of the encoding process previously described. It is the process of transforming words and gestures into thought symbols. Though behavioral scientists are not certain of the exact form in which messages are stored by the brain, most agree that people think in terms of electrochemical nerve impulses or waves.

Responder

The responder is the destination of the originator's message. The term responder implies (1) that a message has been received which is (2) followed by a response. Unless this response (feedback) is made, the communication cycle cannot be considered complete.

In the classroom some responses may be delayed for an extended period, while others may be transmitted immediately after the message has been received and decoded. When delayed responses occur, the originator must be sensitive to this fact and be willing to wait during an incubation period while the response is being formed. Learning theory would suggest that delayed responses should be avoided, when possible, so that oral reinforcement and punishment will be more effective.

The responder has at her or his disposal both verbal and nonverbal response modes. He or she may use these modes in combination or independently. In the classroom setting nonverbal responses are frequently used more than verbal responses. A nod of the head, a gesture of the hand, or a stern look will often provide more effective feedback than will the verbal mode.

Feedback

Self-feedback occurs in intrapersonal communication (1) covertly, through bone conduction, muscular contractions, or neurocircuitry in the central nervous system; and (2) overtly, through the external sensory receptor organs. Feedback also takes place in interpersonal communication. The three types of external feedback available to the originator in interpersonal communication include positive, negative, and ambiguous feedback. Positive feedback occurs when the responder indicates to the originator that he or she understands the message.

Negative feedback means a complete lack of response or a response which indicates that the message is not understood or even received. For example, if the originator asks "What time is it?" and receives the reply "September 22"—this constitutes negative feedback. The response indicates that the originator's message is not correctly decoded and interpreted. Negative feedback, as defined by communication theorists, does not imply disagreement, just a demonstrated lack of understanding.

Ambiguous feedback is that which may be interpreted as either positive or negative feedback by the originator. A blank expression on the responder's face is an example of ambiguous feedback. When ambiguous feedback is interpreted as negative, the originator may find it advantageous to retransmit the message in a different way in order to make it understandable to the responder. Interpretation of ambiguous feedback must be made in light of what the originator knows about the responder and the potential impact of the message being transmitted.

LEVELS OF CLASSROOM COMMUNICATION

Figure 1–2 illustrates the various levels and types of communication which occur in the context of the classroom. While reading this section it might be useful to refer back to it at frequent intervals. Understanding the types and levels of classroom communication is helpful in giving an overview of classroom communication patterns.

Intrapersonal Communication

Intrapersonal communication is that which takes place within the individual. It ranges along a continuum according to the amount of environmental storage required for the message—from thinking, mediating, and reflecting (which require no environmental storage outside the life space of the communicator) to talking aloud to oneself or writing oneself a memo (which require considerably more environmental storage). In the classroom, self-to-self communication will take one of two forms: teacher to self (T—T) or student to self (S_1 —S_1). In each case communication occurs within a single teacher or a single student.

FIGURE 1-2 A Taxonomy of Communication Types and Levels in the Classroom

TYPES AND LEVELS*	ORIGINATOR	TRANSMITTER	CHANNELS	RECEIVER	RESPONDER
I. Intrapersonal A. T—T	Brain-CNS Sensory Organ of Teacher	Brain-CNS Sensory Organ of Teacher	Neural- Thermal- Electrochemical	Brain-CNS Sensory Receptor Organs of Teacher	Brain-CNS Sensory Receptor Organs of Teacher
B. S_1—S_1	Brain-CNS Sensory Organ of $Student_1$	Brain-CNS Sensory Organ of $Student_1$	Neural- Thermal- Electrochemical	Brain-CNS Sensory Receptor Organs of $Student_1$	Brain-CNS Sensory Receptor Organs of $Student_1$
II. Interpersonal A. T—S_1	Brain-CNS of Teacher	Effector Organs of Teacher	Sound Waves, Odor, Heat, etc., or by Mechanical, Chemical, and Kinesthetic Contact	Sensory & Organs of $Student_1$	Brain-CNS of $Student_1$
B. S_1—S_2	Brain-CNS of $Student_1$	Effector Organs of $Student_1$	Sound Waves, Light Waves, Odor, Heat, etc., or by Mechanical, Chemical, and Kinesthetic Contact	Sensory & Organs of $Student_2$	Brain-CNS of $Student_2$

FIGURE 1-2 (continued)

TYPES AND LEVELS*	ORIGINATOR	TRANSMITTER	CHANNELS	RECEIVER	RESPONDER
III. Group A. T—Ss	Brain-CNS of Teacher	Effector Organs of Teacher	Sound Waves, Light Waves, Odor, Heat, etc., or by Mechanical, Chemical, and Kinesthetic Contact	Sensory & Organs of Several Students	Brain-CNS of Several Students
B. Ss—T	Brain-CNS of one or more Students	Spokesman for Students	Sound Waves, Light Waves, Odor, Heat, etc., or by Mechanical, Chemical, and Kinesthetic Contact	Sensory & Organs of Teacher	Brain-CNS of Teacher

	Brain-CNS of Student$_1$	Effector Organs of Student$_1$	Sound Waves, Light Waves, Odor, Heat, etc., or by Mechanical, Chemical, and Kinesthetic Contact	Sensory & Organs of Several Students	Brain-CNS of Several Students
C. S_1——S_s					
IV. Cultural A. C——T_s	Authors, Artists, Educators, Legislators, etc.	Authors, Artists, Educators, Legislators, etc.	Books, Articles, Customs, Written & Unwritten Laws	Teachers & Administrators	Teachers & Administrators
B. C——S_s	Authors, Artists, Educators, Legislators, etc.	Authors, Artists, Educators, Legislators, etc.	Books, Articles, Customs, Written & Unwritten Laws	Students	Students

*Legend: S_1 = Any student
S_2 = Any individual student other than S_1
T = Any teacher
Ss = More than one student in a class
Ts = More than one teacher or administrator in a school system
C = Many persons and/or groups which express moral, educational, or aesthetic views

11

Intrapersonal communication may occur in isolation or in conjunction with higher levels of communication. In most communication settings the intrapersonal level is the basis upon which higher levels of communication operate. Though learning usually takes place as a result of an external stimulus it is primarily intrapersonal in nature.

Two characteristics of intrapersonal communication make it rather unique. First, the originator and responder are within the same individual. Consequently, correction of errors must be made by the individual and not by an outside observer. Secondly, the symbolic form which constitutes the message need only be understood by the individual involved in intrapersonal communication; there is little problem in misinterpretation of language symbols. To illustrate this point, consider the instance when persons who speak two different languages attempt to communicate. Their lack of mutual understanding is primarily a result of their different uses of language symbols to represent the same ideas. Misunderstandings may also occur between people who speak the same language but who attach different meaning to the same word symbols. For example, the word *fast* may mean several different things to different people. In the case of intrapersonal communication, however, one's language code is the same in decoding and encoding stages because only one system of thought symbols is used. As will be discussed later, misinterpretation of word symbols is a major source of communication breakdowns in higher levels of communication.

Interpersonal Communication

Communication on the interpersonal level involves two individuals—an originator and a responder. Unlike intrapersonal communication the originator and responder occupy separate life spaces in the communication environment. Interpersonal communication may occur in any face-to-face encounter and is an important medium of instruction in the classroom. The three forms of interpersonal communication in the classroom are teacher to student $(T—S_1)$, student to teacher $(S_1—T)$, and student to student $(S_1—S_2)$. At this level of communication the message is transmitted to a single student by the teacher, to the teacher by a particular student, or from one student to another student. Examples of interpersonal communication in the classroom include: particular questions about assignments, counseling sessions between student and teacher, team projects between individual students, and teacher-student discussions of seatwork as the teacher moves from desk to desk.

A unique characteristic of interpersonal communication is that both the originator and responder often change roles several times within a communication incident. The originator will initiate a message, the responder will reply, and the originator, in effect, may then respond to the feedback of his initial message. This also implies that the responder must be an active participant in the communication. We must not only receive the message but must respond to it in order for the communication cycle to be completed.

Group Communication

Group communication is probably used more often in the classroom than any other single level of communication. It involves communication between the teacher and several students (T—Ss), between several students and the teacher (Ss—T), or between a single student and several students (S_1—Ss). Examples of group communication in the classroom are class discussions, class recitations, and activities involving group projects. The distinction between interpersonal and group communication is that interpersonal communication takes place between the teacher and a single student or between two students, whereas group communication occurs between many students and the teacher or among several students.

The group communication level is different from other levels in that the flow of messages may be very erratic and have no definite pattern. Spontaneity is a key to successful group communication, but such spontaneity makes careful analysis and organization of the message rather difficult. Because of this characteristic, teachers involved in group communication tend often to structure their presentations tightly and to reduce possible spontaneous discussions which might arise from the presentation. As will be discussed later, this practice not only reduces motivation to learn but actually may inhibit the learning process.

Cultural Communication

Perhaps the most abstract form of classroom communication is found at the cultural level. In cultural communication the originator of the message is often unknown. In most forms of cultural communication there are a number of originators who have helped shape the cultural message. Laws, mores, folkways, and art are all forms of cultural communication. In the classroom the culture communicates to the teachers (C—Ts) as well as to the students (C—Ss). The influence of culture is not restricted to this level of communication but also influences group, interpersonal, and even intrapersonal communication.

Culture dictates moral values, ethical considerations, and educational values which affect perception of the communication setting. In the classroom the subculture of the immediate neighborhood in which the school is located will probably have more influence on students and teachers than the greater cultural concepts held by the nation as a whole. Conflicting subcultures may produce dissonance within communications settings, and such dissonance must be reduced before communication may be completely successful. In a heterogeneous classroom composed of many different races and creeds, the teacher's communications job is more difficult than in a homogeneous community. Though it is occasionally possible to change cultural values through education, it is usually better to try to understand what values are operating in the classroom and adapt to them initially.

In conclusion, communication plays a central role in all classroom activities. The importance of communication, to the teacher, extends beyond the personal considerations and responsibilities of the average citizen. At a variety of different levels, teachers are engaged in training students to become well-balanced citizens in our society. This function of the teacher can only be achieved by focusing on both emotional and social development of students while, at the same time, providing the necessary information and skills to contribute to our socioeconomic systems. This is a considerable charge and one which is primarily accomplished through speech communication—both verbal and nonverbal. The remainder of this text will provide a framework for learning more about the multidimensions of classroom communication. By exploring each chapter it is hoped that your abilities as a classroom communicator will substantially be enhanced.

SUMMARY

Classroom communication is similar to other communication forms but differs as a function of unique purposes, environment, and participation forms. The communication "climate" in the classroom affects the quantity and quality of teacher-student interaction.

The process of classroom communication is dynamic and involves the following components: originator (that is, teacher or student); encoding process (putting the message into appropriate words or movements); transmission (sending messages through specific channels); message (carries meaning from originator to responder via words or movements); channels (the pathways on which messages travel—usually light or sound waves); communication climate (the total of social, hereditary, and personal influences which affect both originator and responder's communication behavior); interference (noise in the communication system which alters or changes meanings of the message); reception (the processing of receiving the message by the eyes, ears, nose, and so on); decoding (the process of transferring the raw aural or visual stimuli into meaningful thought, or word symbols); responder (the person or persons who are the destination of the originator's message); feedback (completes the communication cycle by sending messages back from responder to originator indicating that the message was received and/or understood).

Levels of communication in the classroom include intrapersonal, interpersonal, group, and cultural. Intrapersonal communication takes place within the individual (either teacher or student). Interpersonal communication takes place on a one-to-one basis between a teacher and student or between two students. Group communication takes place in the classroom among a teacher and several students—or within a group of students. Cultural communication reflects the influence of art, literature, laws, mores, and so on on individual communicators. In the classroom this affects both teachers and students.

SUGGESTED READINGS

ALLEN, R. R. and WILLMINGTON, S. CLAY. *Speech Communication in the Secondary School.* Boston: Allyn & Bacon, Inc., 1972.

A primary text for methods courses or proseminars in preparation of teachers of curricular and co-curricular speech communication in American secondary schools, a reference for the new teacher of speech communication and an in-service text for experienced teachers wishing to update knowledges of speech communication instruction.

BROOKS, DEEMS M., (ed.). *Speech Communication Instruction.* New York: David McKay Company, Inc., 1972.

A collection of significant writings concerning communication and instruction, themes carried out within and between themes, summaries of recently developed instructional methods and strategies.

KIBLER, ROBERT J., CEGALA, DONALD, WATSON, KITTIE, BARKER, LARRY, MILES, DAVID. *Objectives for Instruction and Evaluation.* Boston: Allyn & Bacon, Inc., 1981.

A summary of important functions that instructional objectives can serve in improving instruction, including methods of writing instructional objectives, a classroom tested model of instruction, and a variety of material from various sources relating to instructional objectives.

PHILLIPS, GERALD, BUTT, DAVID, METZGER, NANCY. *Communication in Education.* New York: Holt, Rinehart and Winston, Inc., 1974.

A summary of the author's research of communication through teaching, developed set of proposals and methods that would create a climate for learning in school classrooms, regardless of grade level or subject matter taught, methods of teaching children to communicate in classrooms.

REFERENCES

JACKSON, PHILIP W. "Teacher-pupil communication in the elementary classroom: An observational study." Paper presented at the American Educational Research Association Convention, 1965.

SHIPMAN, VIRGINIA C., and ROBERT D. HESS. "Early experience in the socialization of cognitive modes in children: A study of urban negro families." Paper presented at the Fifth Annual Conference of the Family and Society at the Merrill-Palmer Institute, April 1966.

CHAPTER TWO
THE ROLE
AND ASSESSMENT OF
PREREQUISITE BEHAVIORS
IN COMMUNICATION
INSTRUCTION

Donald J. Cegala*

I. Introduction
II. An Approach to the Sequencing of Instruction
   A. Learning Outcomes and Task Analysis
   B. Task Analysis and Preassessment
III. Assessment of Prerequisite Communication Competencies
   A. Interaction Involvement
   B. Assessing Interaction Involvement
   C. Some Observable Dimensions of Interaction Involvement
IV. Summary

*Dr. Cegala is Associate Professor, Department of Communication, at the Ohio State University.

INTRODUCTION

Today teachers of speech communication at all levels of education (that is, elementary through college) are at least familiar with the concept of instructional objectives.[1] Indeed, increasing concern about accountability at all levels of education has been partially responsible for teachers learning how to prepare, implement, and evaluate instructional objectives for a variety of learning outcomes. This chapter is concerned with only certain aspects of instructional objectives—in particular, issues relevant to the sequencing of instructional procedures and experiences that are designed to achieve desired learning outcomes.

However, the major purpose of the chapter is to illustrate how basic research in speech communication may be applied in classroom settings. Often there is an unfortunate communication gap between basic researchers and classroom teachers. This chapter, hopefully, will show that such gaps are not necessary.

The first part of the chapter focuses on concepts that are especially relevant to classroom decision making. In particular, desired learning outcomes are examined with respect to a procedure called task analysis. The procedure is illustrated and discussed in relation to how it can aid teachers in sequencing learning outcomes for a given unit of instruction.

A discussion of task analysis leads to a concern about students' entry competencies—that is, the capabilities that students have prior to the instruction which is to occur in a given unit or course. The concept of preassessment is examined in this context, suggesting that teachers may want to evaluate students' entry competencies with respect to the sequencing procedures indicated by a task analysis. The pragmatics of this procedure are examined, suggesting that it is not always possible to identify and assess all of the relevant prerequisite competencies necessary for instruction. It is implied that teachers, out of practical necessity, may often assume that students are capable of base level prerequisite behaviors rather than attempting to assess these behaviors directly (for example, adequate listening skills and a positive attitude about communicating). While this is a practical solution to a difficult problem, an alternative procedure is offered here. In particular, it is suggested that teachers assess students' fundamental communication competencies with various instruments that are already available in the literature. In effect, this alternative underscores the importance of the relationship between basic research and instruction in speech communication. This point is illustrated by selecting one type of prerequisite competency as an example and indicating how it can be assessed by the use of a paper and pencil questionnaire. In addition to the questionnaire, various overt manifestations of the basic competency are examined in reference to general behavior patterns (for example, socially appropriate behavior) and specific nonverbal behaviors (for example, eye gaze).

[1]Some individuals may use other terms such as behavioral objectives or performance goals.

AN APPROACH TO THE
SEQUENCING OF INSTRUCTION

Learning Outcomes and Task Analysis

In 1963, Professor Kibler introduced the now familiar concept of instructional objectives to professionals in speech communication. Later he headed a research team that produced several journal articles about instructional objectives and their role in speech communication education (Kibler, Barker, & Cegala 1970a; Kibler, Barker, & Cegala 1970b; Cegala and others 1972). This work was based on an instructional model that was initially described in the book *Behavioral Objectives and Instruction* (Kibler, Barker, & Miles 1970) and later revised under the title *Objectives for Instruction and Evaluation* (Kibler and others 1974). This book is now in a second edition (Kibler and others 1981).

Kibler and others (1981) define an instructional objective as "statements that describe what students will be able to do after completing a prescribed unit of instruction" (p. 2). It is of critical importance that the instructional objective writer specify what *observable behaviors* students are to demonstrate before mastery of the objective is achieved. For example, the following objective does not clearly indicate an observable behavior: *The student will know how to organize a speech.* The term "know" is ambiguous. It does not specify in observable terms how the student is to demonstrate mastery. In contrast, the following objective provides this needed specificity: *Given a randomly ordered set of paragraphs of a speech, the student will reorder them in writing to conform to one of the four major organizing principles discussed in the textbook.* Note the specificity in this objective regarding what the student is to do. The student is to produce a written product which is a reordered, organized version of the paragraphs.[2]

While the observable behavior specification is not the only component of an instructional objective (see Kibler and others 1981; Cegala and others 1972), it is certainly an important aspect. The observable behavior identified in an instructional objective is often called a *learning outcome;* it is what is desired on the part of the learner after a given unit of instruction. It perhaps goes without saying that the writer of instructional objectives must have a clear idea of the learning outcomes desired before objectives can be prepared.

Of course, all competent teachers have a notion of which learning out-

---

[2]There are, of course, varying philosophies about the use of instructional objectives, including whether they should be used at all (see Kibler and others 1974). While there is no intention to neglect the importance of these philosophical differences, it is not possible or appropriate to address them in this chapter. It is assumed here that most approaches to instruction involve some minimum content that must be acquired by learners if they are to progress in the learning process. Instructional objectives are often useful to teachers and students for all or most of this type of content because they clearly communicate instructional intentions to relevant persons in the educational process. Even so, it should be understood that a commitment to use instructional objectives for part of the instructional process does not necessarily commit a teacher to employ them for the entire process or to specify all of the important desired learning outcomes in an instructional objective format.

comes they are trying to achieve in the classroom. However, there are an infinite variety of learning outcomes that may be sought by educators, parents, and students. Because of this diversity in potentially desirable learning outcomes, it is useful for teachers to specify those outcomes that are most relevant to given units of instruction. By specifying learning outcomes, teachers can more effectively communicate their intentions to each other, to parents, and to students.

Because learning outcomes are so important to instruction, educators have spent considerable time developing schemes to aid in classifying various types of outcomes into more clearly defined clusters, or groupings (for example, Bloom and others 1956; Krathwohl, Bloom, & Masia 1964; Gagné 1977; Simpson 1972). Space does not permit an examination of these schemes here, but the reader is encouraged to examine one or more of them. A summary of selected schemes and their use is presented in Kibler and others (1974; 1981).

While it is important and useful to classify desired learning outcomes according to some common dimension(s), classification alone is typically not enough to provide maximum use of instructional objectives. The teacher must also be concerned with sequencing the objectives to maximize the efficiency and effectiveness of learning experiences. This chapter is concerned with this particular aspect of instructional objectives.

The task of sequencing instructional units to maximize learning is sometimes one of the most interesting and creative challenges a teacher faces in designing classroom instruction. While perhaps not often recognized as such, it seems analogous to theory building in scientific endeavors. The teacher must construct a coherent stream of ideas and experiences by adding together bits and pieces of information. Oftentimes one is not sure if initial sequencing decisions are good ones until the instructional unit is actually taught. As students' learning is observed and assessed, more information is acquired so that revisions can be made before the unit is taught again. While it is probably true that the ultimate test of sequencing decisions rests with actual classroom implementation over a period of time, it is of course desirable to maximize the effectiveness of sequencing decisions prior to implementation. How can this maximization be achieved?

The manner in which instructional units are sequenced is partially (if not largely) related to the nature of the content being taught. However, there are some basic principles of learning that generalize to most content areas and allow for guidance in the sequencing of instructional objectives. One such learning principle relates to the hierarchical arrangement of content material (Gagné 1977). All teachers know that learning new material is often importantly related to the acquisition of prerequisite competencies. In other words, instructional units typically are sequenced so that the fundamentals are taught first, gradually leading to the more difficult and complex material.[3] When this type of sequenc-

---

[3]Although this appears to be a general rule of teaching, it should be noted that some content areas do not require sequential, hierarchical ordering, and such sequencing is not possible or appropriate for other content areas.

ing is used to order desired learning outcomes, a procedure called task analysis is often quite useful (Gagné & Briggs 1974; Gagné 1977).

Task analysis is a procedure for breaking down a complex behavior into its component parts. While it is by no means an easy procedure, its logic is reasonably straightforward. One begins with the terminal behavior (that is, the learning outcome desired for a given unit of instruction) and asks: *What does the learner have to be able to do in order to accomplish this?* The answer(s) to this question helps to identify what necessary competencies are needed to perform the desired learning outcome. Of course, one does not typically complete a task analysis with just one question. Usually the key question is repeated several times until the terminal behavior is broken down into as many component parts as possible for practical purposes. For example, consider the task analysis in figure 2-1.

The terminal objective is located at the top of figure 2-1 (that is, *Able to Write a Well-Organized Message*). The first row of necessary competencies indicates the responses derived from the first time the key question was asked. Note, however, that these learning outcomes are of a rather complex nature themselves—they involve the application of rules and principles of organization. Because these behaviors are also rather complex, the key question was asked again; the responses are in row two. It can be seen that the learning outcomes in row one are dependent upon the learning outcomes in row two. For example, in order to apply rules for writing central ideas, the learner must be able to discrimi-

FIGURE 2-1   Task Analysis for a Complex Objective

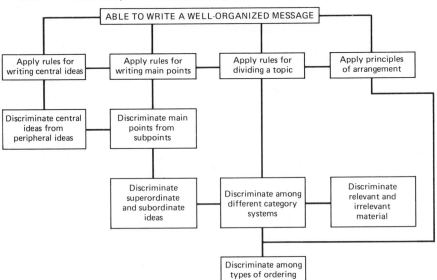

Note: See Haynes (1973) for more complete information on rules and concepts related to message organization.

nate central ideas from peripheral ones (that is, he or she must understand what a central idea is).[4] Similarly, the key question was asked again and again to obtain the remaining rows in the task analysis. Of course, it is possible to continue asking the key question beyond the point where the analysis ends in figure 2-1. Where one stops in the analysis depends in part upon what can be assumed on the part of learners. In other words, one ends the task analysis at the point where all students can demonstrate the row of behaviors indicated. This point will be addressed more specifically in subsequent sections of this chapter.

It should be clear that task analysis is a useful procedure to employ in designing instruction. Among other things, it provides considerable guidance for sequencing units of instruction in a hierarchical manner. When task analysis is employed prior to instruction, the teacher is less likely to leave out important steps in the sequence of instructional content—steps that are necessary to master the terminal objective. At the same time, task analysis aids in grouping instructional objectives that require similar prerequisite competencies, thus further aiding in the sequencing of units of instruction. Sometimes this sequencing provides direction in selecting or developing instructional strategies and materials. Although there are no conclusive research findings about which instructional strategy is most effective for achieving given levels of learner outcomes, knowledge of the specific level one is attempting to achieve and how it relates to other learning outcomes provides a good basis for making intelligent decisions about instruction strategies (see Gagné 1977). Task analysis is also useful in relation to the evaluation of learning outcomes. For example, a student's performance on an assessment procedure (for example, a test) may be examined in light of the hierarchical sequence of learning outcomes to determine where (in the task analysis) the student is having difficulty. Such assessment may provide insight into why the difficulty arose and/or how it may be corrected.

Task Analysis and Preassessment

While task analysis has many uses, the one of primary interest here is related to the sequencing of instructional units. The general way that task analysis aids in sequencing instruction was illustrated and discussed in the preceding section. In this section the concern about sequencing will be narrowed to focus on the initial stages of learning for a prescribed unit of instruction.

Recall that a task analysis ideally is terminated when one reaches the level of behavior that *all* learners are already able to demonstrate. However, as any teacher knows, students begin instructional units with various backgrounds and experiences with the content. It is, therefore, difficult to assume where instruction of new material should begin. Accordingly, preassessment of learners is

---

[4]It is important to note that applying rules means more than just being able to recite rules. The learner must be able to *use* a rule effectively. Mere reciting of a rule would be considered a low-level behavior—that is, one several rows down from the terminal objective.

often used in conjunction with task analysis. As the term suggests, preassessment is an evaluation procedure used prior to beginning a prescribed unit of instruction. It determines (1) whether students have the prerequisite competencies for the instruction to follow, (2) how much of what is to be learned is already known, and (3) the instructional experiences that should be presented to each student (Kilber and others 1981).

The relationship between preassessment and task analysis is intimate. Ideally, the preassessment evaluation should represent each stage in the task analysis so that all of the critical behaviors are assessed. In this manner, a teacher may use the results of preassessment to determine where each student is in the task analysis hierarchy. This information would then provide the basis for determining where instruction should begin and how it should proceed. For example, preassessment designed for the task analysis in figure 2–1 might consist of a written test that begins with a few items which assess students' ability to discriminate among types of ordering. Subsequent items would include assessments of students' ability to discriminate superordinate and subordinate ideas, different category systems, relevant and irrelevant material, and so on up the hierarchy until all of the critical behaviors were tested. The results of this testing would allow the teacher to place each student somewhere in the hierarchy, thus providing valuable information about how to adapt instructional procedures to each individual or to groups of students.[5]

While the combined use of task analysis and preassessment is valuable for designing and implementing instruction, it is not free of drawbacks. First, preassessment should ideally be conducted for each new major unit of instruction for which no prior information about students' competencies is available. Typically, teachers do not have the time to develop such elaborate assessment procedures. Second, task analysis is typically a time-consuming procedure, although the initial time spent on developing the analysis is usually well worth the effort. Third, task analysis is most appropriate for content that can be arranged or analyzed hierarchically. It is not particularly useful for other types of content. Fourth, it is sometimes difficult to determine just where a task analysis should end (that is, what competencies should one assume that all learners are capable of doing). If the task analysis does not include all of the behaviors that are relevant to the terminal objective, then a preassessment based on the analysis may fail to show where some students are experiencing difficulty with the subject matter. This problem is of particular interest here, and the remainder of the chapter is devoted to an examination of it.

---

[5] If there are no means available for individualized instruction the preassessment results are still valuable for adapting initial instruction to the entire class.

ASSESSMENT OF PREREQUISITE
COMMUNICATION COMPETENCIES

Clearly it is not practical to extend each task analysis to the lowest-level prerequisite behaviors that may have relevance to the terminal objective. For example, in theory the task analysis in figure 2-1 could be extended to fundamental language skills, such as ordering words into sentences, sentences into paragraphs, and even more basic skills. Rather than including these kinds of basic skills in the task analysis, teachers typically assume that all learners have some base level of competency and end the task analysis at that point. Although this is one practical way to solve the problem of where to end a task analysis, it may not always be the best approach. It is possible that some learners may not have acquired even the most basic skills needed for a given unit of instruction. Of course, this state of affairs is undesirable for any instructional endeavor, whether or not it is sequenced according to a task analysis.

The difficulties created by the lack of necessary prerequisite competencies are especially problematic when assumed to be part of a learner's repertoire simply on the basis of his or her age. Flavell (1972) and others (see Bassett, Whittington, & Staton-Spicer 1979) have suggested that it is erroneous to assume that even adults necessarily demonstrate fundamental behaviors that are typically acquired during earlier stages of development. If this is true of adults, it would also seem likely for younger learners.

At the moment, researchers in speech communication are developing ways of measuring basic communication competencies that will greatly aid the classroom teacher in identifying learners who lack certain fundamental skills (see Del Polito 1979). These assessment instruments will probably not preclude the need for teachers to develop their own preassessment procedures for specific learning hierarchies, but they will aid teachers in preassessing the kind of fundamental communication competencies that may now often be assumed to be part of the learners' repertoire. The remainder of this chapter will focus on an assessment instrument that illustrates the kind of fundamental prerequisite communication behaviors that may be important for teachers to preassess. Teachers of interpersonal and small group communication may find the instrument especially relevant to their needs, although some research on the instrument suggests that it may have relevance to communication competence in other settings, including the mass media (Ross 1978).

Interaction Involvement

The assessment of fundamental communication competencies has been a research emphasis of this author for some time (see Cegala & Bassett 1976). One of the products of that research is a paper-and-pencil questionnaire which assesses the extent of an individual's *interaction involvement* during face-to-face communication (Cegala 1978; 1981). Interaction involvement is composed of two fundamental communication behaviors—attentiveness and perceptiveness. However, before examining these dimensions of interaction involvement, it may be useful to discuss what is meant by the general term. Interaction involvement is defined as *the extent to which an individual partakes in a social environment.* The definition implies that involved individuals engage in more active participation with the social environment than do less involved individuals. Yet, the exact meaning of "active participation with the social environment" may require additional clarification.

When an individual is highly involved in an interaction, his or her active participation is focused on an accounting of (1) other's behavior and (2) how other is perceiving self. Herbert Blumer (1953) provides an exceptionally lucid description of this process.

> . . . Taking another person into account means more than merely being in his presence or merely responding to him . . . Taking another person into account means being aware of him, identifying him in some way, making some judgment or appraisal of him, identifying the meaning of his action, trying to find out what he has on his mind or trying to figure out what he intends to do. Such awareness of another person in this sense of taking him and his acts into consideration becomes the occasion for orienting oneself and for the direction of one's own conduct. One takes the other person and his action into account not merely at the point of initial contact, but actually throughout the period of interaction. One has to keep abreast of the action of the other, noting what he says at this point and that point or interpreting his movements as they appear, one after another. Perceiving, defining and judging the other person and his action and organizing oneself in terms of such definitions and judgments constitute a continuing or running process (p. 194).

The ongoing account of self and other is a function of how inner feelings, thoughts, and experiences are directed to and integrated with the various phenomena of the social environment (especially others' behavior). This kind of participation with the social environment requires several kinds of capabilities, among them attentiveness and perceptiveness. One's attentiveness to objects and people in the immediate environment allows for the acquisition of information that is necessary to adapt one's own behavior to the demands of the situation. Similarly, one's perceptiveness, or understanding of the social context of which one is part, also allows for appropriate, adaptive behavior. Accordingly, attentiveness and perceptiveness appear to be fundamentally important facets of the ongoing accounting process of self and other that was described above. The term *interaction involvement* is used here in reference to the general tendency to demonstrate both attentiveness and perceptiveness in social interactions. These concepts are discussed more completely in the following sections.

Attentiveness. Everyone probably has some intuitive understanding that attentiveness is fundamental to competent interpersonal communication. Yet, it is also probably true that everyone becomes inattentive to some extent during the course of interacting with others. For example, it is not uncommon for a listener to become momentarily preoccupied with thoughts about events unrelated to a conversation even while overtly behaving in a manner to suggest that he or she is still listening to the speaker. In fact, most people seem to learn how to time various listener responses (for example, "yes," "uh-huh," "really") to suggest to the speaker that full attention is being given, when in fact little or no listening is taking place.

Although inattentiveness is typically attributed to the listener in the communication process, it can also apply to a speaker. For instance, speakers sometimes fail to attend to listener responses which suggest that some corrective behavior is needed on their part (for example, failing to see a look of confusion on a listener's face). In either case, the potential result is the same—the inattentive communicator is likely to lose sense of what is taking place in the conversation. Stated differently, the individual may become unaware of the presumed relationship between self, other, and situation, thus resulting in misunderstanding, embarrassment, and/or violation of expectations for appropriate behavior.

While even momentary inattentiveness is at the very least impolite, everyone seems to be subject to it to some degree. To this extent, occasional inattentiveness may be considered "natural" to human communication and reasonably tolerated. However, when individuals become *characteristically* inattentive during their interpersonal communications, it is an entirely different matter. These individuals often experience considerable difficulty in relating to others and may even be perceived as being generally socially incompetent. Some of the ways this social incompetence is manifested will be discussed in more detail later on.

Perceptiveness. While attentiveness is fundamentally important to competent interpersonal communication, it alone does not account for complete involvement in conversation. Perceptiveness is also needed for adequate interaction involvement. Perceptiveness refers to the extent to which an individual is sensitive to what meanings ought to be placed on others' behavior and what meanings others have placed on his or her own behavior (Goffman 1967). While perceptiveness is dependent upon attentiveness, it should be clear that one can be attentive but not necessarily perceptive. Perceptiveness requires more than just attending to cues in the social environment—it requires the attribution and integration of meanings associated with those cues and an appropriate response to them. In other words, perceptiveness is the extent to which an individual understands and responds to the symbolic relationship between self and other, that relationship constituting the social reality of the immediate situation.[6]

Attentiveness and perceptiveness during interpersonal communication encounters is called interaction involvement. An individual who typically demonstrates a high degree of attentiveness and perceptiveness is considered high in interaction involvement. It is important to emphasize that interaction involvement may be viewed in at least two ways. First, interaction involvement may be viewed as an ongoing, process phenomenon that may change continuously throughout a given interaction. As suggested already, most communicators probably have experienced varying degrees of involvement in particular interactions. However, interaction involvement may be viewed in a second way that is less a function of factors operating in a particular communication event—for example, an individual may feel especially preoccupied with a personal problem, a communicator is especially difficult to follow, the situation is new to a person and he or she is having difficulty adapting to it. Viewed in this second way, interaction involvement is a general orientation toward the act of communicating. Those individuals who demonstrate a highly involved general orientation toward the act of communicating are people who assume an attentive-perceptive posture for all or most of their interactions across a variety of situations. In a sense, involvement becomes part of their style of communicating (see Norton 1978) and is assumed as a natural part of the communicative act. Indeed, a high interaction involvement orientation may be so natural to some people that they may have difficulty understanding the perspective of low-involved individuals. Rather than being assumed quite naturally, attentiveness and perceptiveness for less involved people are difficult to maintain during many or most conversations without considerable effort.

Assessing Interaction Involvement

Of particular concern here is the tendency to assume that most learners demonstrate attentiveness and perceptiveness at a level sufficient for competent interpersonal communication. As will be seen shortly, such an assumption may be quite erroneous even when the learners are adults. Accordingly, it would appear useful to have some means for preassessing the extent to which individuals demonstrate involvement during their interactions with others. Such an assessment could provide valuable information about a learner's prerequisite competency prior to instruction in such courses as interpersonal and small group communication.

[6] There is rather extensive literature on what is meant here by constituted social reality (for example, see Berger & Luckmann 1967; Filmer and others 1972; Mehan & Wood 1975). Suffice it to say that it refers to the sense of who one is and what is happening socially at a moment in time.

The items that comprise the interaction involvement scale are reported in table 2-1. These items are the result of considerable research over several years (see Cegala 1981). While the involvement scale is by no means perfect, it can be used as an initial screening instrument to assess learners' general tendencies toward attentiveness and perceptiveness in their interpersonal communications.

TABLE 2-1   The Interaction Involvement Scale[1]

SCALE ITEMS[2]

1. I am keenly aware of how others perceive me during my conversations. (P)[3]
2. My mind wanders during conversations and I often miss parts of what is going on. (A)
3. Often in conversations I'm not sure what to say, I cannot seem to find the appropriate lines. (P)
4. I carefully observe how others respond to me during my conversations. (P)
5. Often I will pretend to be listening to someone when in fact I'm thinking about something else. (A)
6. Often in conversations I'm not sure what my role is; that is, I'm not sure how I'm expected to relate to others. (P)
7. I listen carefully to others during a conversation. (A)
8. Often I am preoccupied in my conversations and do not pay complete attention to others. (A)
9. Often in conversations I'm not sure what the other is *really* saying. (P)
10. Often in conversations I am not sure what others' needs (e.g., reassurance, a compliment, etc.) are until it is too late to respond appropriately. (P)
11. During conversations I am sensitive to others' subtle or hidden meanings. (P)
12. I am very observant during my conversations with others. (A)
13. In conversations I pay close attention to what others say and do and try to obtain as much information as I can. (A)
14. Often I feel sort of "unplugged" from the social situation of which I am part; that is, I'm uncertain of my role, others' motives, and what's happening. (P)
15. In my conversations, I really know what's going on; that is, I have a "handle on the situation." (P)
16. In my conversations, I can accurately perceive others' intentions quite well. (P)
17. Often in conversations I'm not sure how I'm expected to respond. (P)
18. In conversations I am responsive to the meaning of others' behavior in relation to myself and the situation. (P)

---

[1] The questionnaire is administered with the following directions: "This questionnaire is designed to provide information about how people communicate. There are no right or wrong answers to any of the questions. You only need to indicate the extent to which you feel that each questionnaire item describes *your own behavior.* In responding to some of the questionnaire items, you might say, 'sometimes I do and sometimes I don't.' You should respond to each questionnaire item in a way that best describes your general manner of behavior; that is, how you tend to respond in most situations. If you cannot decide how a particular item applies to you, then mark the 'not sure' alternative. However, try to be careful and thoughtful in making all your responses."

[2] The following scale is placed below each item on the questionnaire: Not at all like me; Not like me. Somewhat unlike me; Not sure; Somewhat like me; Like me; Very much like me. For scoring purposes, the scale values are 1-7 beginning with 1 for "Not at all like me."

[3] The A or P after the items indicates attentiveness and perceptiveness, respectively.

Table 2-1 contains most of the information needed to employ the inter-action involvement scale. The directions should be placed on a cover sheet, followed by the 18 items in the order given in table 2-1. The letters in parenthesis after each item should be omitted. These are included only for interpretation purposes. The format that has been used for the questionnaire is as follows:

1. I am keenly aware of how others perceive me during my conversations.
    | Not at all | Not like | Somewhat | Not sure | Somewhat | Like | Very much |
    | like me | me | unlike me | | like me | me | like me |
2. My mind wanders during conversations and I often miss parts of what is going on.
    | Not at all | Not like | Somewhat | Not sure | Somewhat | Like | Very much |
    | like me | me | unlike me | | like me | me | like me |
3. etc.

As indicated in table 2-1, the scale values range from 1 to 7 beginning with "Not at all like me." This method of scoring will result in higher total scores meaning greater involvement *if* the following items are reversed: 2, 3, 5, 6, 8, 9, 10, 14, 17.[7]

Of course, any type of measurement procedure is subject to error. This is no less true for the interaction involvement questionnaire and, therefore, some degree of caution should be exercised in interpreting scores. Some guidelines are available, however, to aid in interpretation, but these are based primarily on responses of college students and should cautiously be applied to other types of respondents.

The guidelines for interpreting college students' responses to the involvement questionnaire are based on a sample of 1,187 students at Ohio State University. These students ranged from freshmen to seniors and represented majors from diverse areas of study. There were approximately equal numbers of males and females in the sample. Table 2-2 contains relevant information about the involvement scores obtained for three samples of individuals.[8] At the moment, attention is focused only on the college student sample.

As indicated in table 2-2, the mean involvement score for the college student sample was 90.56. Dividing this mean by the number of items on the

[7]For example, if a respondent indicates "Not at all like me" to item 2, instead of receiving an item score of 1, he or she should receive a score of 7. This is because item 2 (and the others listed above) is phrased in the negative. In effect, reversing the scale values on these items changes them to positively phrased items and allows for a simple addition of the 18-item scores to arrive at a total score on the involvement questionnaire. It is extremely important to reverse the scoring on one-half of the items or the total added score across the 18 items will not be accurate.

It is also possible to compute subtest scores for attentiveness and perceptiveness by adding the appropriate item scores as indicated in table 2-1. However, for general screening purposes, a single interaction involvement score is easier to work with and serves quite well.

[8]These and all other data reported here were obtained following the scoring procedures outlined earlier.

TABLE 2-2 Descriptive Statistics on College, High School, and Nonstudent Adults

DESCRIPTOR	COLLEGE	HIGH SCHOOL	NONSTUDENT ADULT
sample size	1187	78	78
mean	90.56	86.33	89.12
standard deviation	14.45	15.69	15.96
min./max. score	18/114	21/89	19/89
skewness	− .334	.119	− .074
kurtosis	.127	.465	.612
percent scoring above the mean	49	50	49
percent scoring below the mean	48	50	48
internal reliability	.89	.88	.93

questionnaire (or, 18) translates it to the original 1-7 scale. This computation results in a score of 5.03, which is almost exactly at "somewhat like me." The distribution about this mean is reasonably normal, although there is some negative skewness and slight peakedness.

Earlier it was suggested that individuals demonstrate less attentiveness and perceptiveness during interpersonal communications than may often be assumed. The data based on 1,187 college students tend to support this claim. Slightly more than one-half of the sample (that is, 608 respondents—51%) report that they generally are somewhat or less involved in their interpersonal communications. Of course, the context in which the communication occurs may be expected to influence the extent of most individuals' involvement. However, some preliminary data on this topic suggest that there is little or no difference in individuals' general involvement level when talking with friends, acquaintances, roommates, parents, or relatives.[9] More will be said later about the manifestation of involvement in specific situations. For now, attention is turned to the data from the high school and nonstudent adult samples reported in table 2-2.

Overall, the data across the three samples of respondents appear remarkably comparable. However, it must be emphasized that the samples of high school and nonstudent adults are quite small and probably not widely representative. There is only one statistically significant difference among the means of the involvement scores. The college sample mean is significantly higher than the high school sample mean ($t=2.486$, $df=1263$, $p<.05$, two tailed). At first glance this result may lead one to hypothesize that education level or age may account for the difference. However, this interpretation is not warranted by the data. At this time it is not clear whether the observed difference between the college and high

[9] These findings are based on a subset of the 1,187 college students. There were 184 students in the sample. They completed the involvement questionnaire twice, once as the items applied to their behavior in most conversations, and once as the items applied to the first conversation of that day. In addition, students indicated who they engaged in the conversation.

school groups is a function of sampling error or some systematic factor yet unknown. More data are required to determine if the differences reported here are reliable and, if so, what factors may account for them. Although caution must be exercised in interpreting the data reported in table 2-2, the general comparability across the three samples lends support to the speculation that individuals may demonstrate relatively lower involvement across communication encounters than what may be initially expected.

Some Observable Dimensions of Interaction Involvement

The role of observable behaviors was emphasized early in the chapter when discussing instructional objectives and their relationship to learning outcomes and the sequencing of instruction. At this point it may be useful to examine the concept of interaction involvement in terms of observable behaviors. The following discussion is designed to aid teachers in (1) identifying students who may experience difficulty in being involved during interactions, and/or (2) preparing objectives or alternative preassessment procedures for evaluating students' interaction involvement. The discussion is presented in two phases. First, interaction involvement is related to other general response tendencies that teachers often observe in students (for example, self confidence). Second, involvement is discussed in relation to several nonverbal behaviors that seem indicative of differing levels of interaction involvement.

Involvement and related general tendencies. A sample of 370 college students completed the involvement questionnaire along with several other paper and pencil instruments.[10] After completing the questionnaires the sample was divided into high-, medium-, and low-involvement groups.[11] These groups were then compared on their responses to the other questionnaires. In terms of self-concept, the low-involvement group scored significantly lower than the medium- or high-involvement groups on two dimensions of self-esteem.[12] First, the low-involvement group indicated that they perceived themselves to be less fun to be with socially, less popular than others of the same age, and generally less well liked than most other people. Second, the low-involvement group reported a significantly more negative self-image than the other groups. For example, they

---

[10]The other instruments were a self-esteem questionnaire (Coopersmith 1967), an assertiveness questionnaire (Galassi and others 1974), and a questionnaire designed to measure extraversion and neuroticism (Eysenck 1973).

[11]This was done by adding and subtracting one standard deviation to the mean and treating all the scores within that interval as medium involvement. There were 55 high scores, 58 low scores, and 257 medium scores.

[12]On the basis of norms established from the sample of 1,187, the low-involvement group includes people who scored 75 or below. The high-involvement group includes people who scored 106 or above, while the medium group includes people who scored between 76 and 105. These cutoff points may serve as guidelines when using the involvement questionnaire with college students. However, it is best to compute the mean and standard deviation on any sample that responds to the questionnaire.

indicated a greater desire to be someone else, felt as though they were not as nice looking as most people, and generally had a low opinion of themselves.

All three groups differed significantly from one another in terms of general temperament. The three types of temperament that were involved in these differences were choleric, melancholic, and sanguine (see Eysenck 1973). The choleric temperament was characterized by the following adjectives: irritable, restless, aggressive, excitable, changeable, impulsive, active. The melancholic temperament was characterized as moody, anxious, nervous, sober, unsociable, quiet, pessimistic. The sanguine temperament was sociable, outgoing, talkative, responsive, lively, carefree. The low-involvement group scored significantly higher on choleric and melancholic temperaments than either the medium- or high-involvement groups.[13] This suggests a relationship between low involvement and neuroticism, or degree of emotionality (see Roback 1927; Eysenck 1947; Eysenck & Eysenck 1969). Also, the low-involvement group scored significantly lower on sanguine temperament than the high-involvement group. Overall, these data suggest that low-involvement individuals tend to demonstrate choleric and melancholic temperaments, and tend not to demonstrate sanguine temperament. In short, these data suggest that low-involvement people are less emotionally stable. Accordingly, low-involvement people are likely to demonstrate anxious behavior in many social contexts.

Perhaps of particular use to teachers of speech communication are the data relating interaction involvement with the demonstration of generally socially appropriate behavior. In this case, the definition of socially appropriate behavior was derived from research in assertiveness training (Wolpe & Lazarus 1966; Wolpe 1969). This approach defines socially appropriate behavior as the ability to express justified negative and positive feelings toward others. Negative expressions include justified anger, disagreement, dissatisfaction, and annoyance, while positive expressions include feelings of love, affection, admiration, approval, and agreement. Individuals who are able to express these positive and negative feelings to others when justified are expected to be generally better adjusted to the social environment. In particular, they are expected to adapt readily to social situations, exert some control over the social environment—but not in a domineering, aggressive manner—and establish open, stable relationships with others. These appear to be among many important behaviors that speech communication teachers strive to instill and nurture in their students. Accordingly, it is of particular interest that the data indicate a strong relationship between interaction involvement scores and the tendency to behave in a socially appropriate manner. All three involvement groups differed significantly on social appropriateness, with the low-involvement group scoring lowest, followed by the medium group, and then by the high-involvement group.

Overall, the data based on responses from 370 college students suggest that

---

[13]These groups also scored significantly different, with the medium group scoring higher than the high-involvement group.

high-involvement individuals are more likely to demonstrate greater self-esteem, more carefree and less irritable and anxious temperament, and greater frequency of socially appropriate behavior. In general, more highly involved individuals may be expected to be better adjusted to the social environment and experience far less difficulty in establishing relationships with others.

However, it would be a mistake to rely only on scores from the interaction involvement questionnaire to make assessments about students' potential communication difficulties. There may be a discrepancy between a respondent's score on the involvement questionnaire and the extent of actual involvement demonstrated at a particular time or during a certain type of communication context (for example, at school, at home). Accordingly, it is important to use the interaction involvement scores in conjunction with careful observation of students' behavior during their interactions with others. While research is currently underway to identify some of the specific communication behaviors associated with involvement, some preliminary findings are available at this time. These findings may help to identify variance in interaction involvement during interactions with students.

Involvement and related nonverbal behaviors. Cegala, Alexander, and Sokuvitz (1979) reported initial findings that suggested low interaction involvement was associated with less eye gaze while speaking and listening. Since that initial report, subsequent research findings have supported the relationship, especially for males. Intuitively, these findings make sense as eye gaze aversion has been found to indicate various forms of turning inward (see Exline & Fehr 1978; Harper, Wiens, & Matarazzo 1978). As described earlier, low interaction involvement suggests a turning inward, whereby an individual focuses on some aspect of the inner, personal world while participation with the external world is lessened to some degree.

The definition of low interaction involvement as a turning inward phenomenon suggested that it might be associated with certain types of gesturing. Freedman (1972) and his associates have identified two categories of gesturing that seem to reflect relative degrees of inward versus outward orientation on the part of an individual. Gestures that reflect an inward orientation are called body-focused movements. They include various forms of gesturing that involve contact with one's own body or some external object. The forms of body-focused gesturing include continuous hand to hand movement, hand to body movement and hand to object movement (for example, clothing, a pen). According to Freedman, body-focused gestures indicate a split in attention between self and other, suggesting an inward orientation on the part of the person engaged in body-focused movement. This hypothesis seems to have some intuitive support. For example, the reader might take note of his or her thoughts the next time body-focused gesturing is done during a conversation. It is likely that you will be experiencing some form of preoccupation with inner thoughts, feelings, or experiences that will exclude concern about the immediate external world.

In contrast to body-focused gesturing is what Freedman (1972) calls object-focused gesturing. These movements are directed away from the body and toward the other. They are tied directly to speech, unlike body-focused gestures which may occur during speaking or listening. Included in the object-focused category are punctuating movements, illustrators, and other forms of gesturing that seem to enhance the spoken word, presumably for the benefit of the listener. For example, if someone is describing an object, he or she may use several gestures to indicate the shape and size of it so the listener can understand the message better. According to Freedman, such gestures are indicative of the speaker's intent to enhance his or her message and are, therefore, indicative of an outward, communicative orientation on the part of the speaker.

Following the logic of body-focused versus object-focused gesturing, individuals' gestures were coded into three categories during an informal conversation. It was found that low-interaction-involvement individuals demonstrated significantly more body-focused gestures during their conversations than higher-involved individuals (Cegala 1978). A second study produced results similar to those found in the first study, especially for females. Individuals who scored highly on interaction involvement demonstrated significantly less body-focused gestures and more object-focused gestures than low-involvement people during informal conversations with strangers. Overall, these findings suggest that body-focused geatures may be indicative of low interaction involvement, while object focused gestures may indicate higher involvement.

Finally, various types of speech disfluencies have been examined in relation to interaction involvement. Initial findings (Cegala and others 1978) suggested that lower involvement was associated with a greater frequency of vocalized pausing (for example, "ah," "hum"). Subsequent research was less supportive of this initial finding, but there is a tendency for low-involvement males to demonstrate more sentence changes—for example, "May I . . . Tell me something, are you telling the truth?" and "you knows" during informal conversations with strangers.

Observations of these and related behaviors should be considered in conjunction with involvement questionnaire scores in making assessments of individuals. In addition, observations of general behavior tendencies such as self-esteem level, temperament, and social appropriateness may be useful to integrate with other information about involvement. Often teachers are able to acquire accurate information about such general behavior tendencies during the normal course of communication with students over a period of time. These observations and subsequent assessments are a valuable source of information to aid the teacher in relating to students and helping them with various communication difficulties.

No paper-and-pencil questionnaire can substitute for the kind of information acquired from direct, personal contact with students. However, the data from the interaction involvement questionnaire may be useful in the initial idenfication of students who may have potential difficulty in demonstrating attentiveness and perceptiveness during their interpersonal communications. Such information may be quite valuable to the teacher in at least the early stages of a course in planning instructional strategies—dividing the class into work groups, selecting simulations and games, choosing "volunteers" for classroom instruction. Of course, interaction involvement is not the only potentially important fundamental communication competency on which to assess students. It has been emphasized here as an illustration of the kind of prerequisite competency that may be important to consider when planning and sequencing instruction. Hopefully, continued basic research on human communication will provide the means for identifying and assessing several fundamental competencies that will aid the classroom teacher in a variety of instructionally related decisions.

SUMMARY

This chapter has covered considerable material in a relatively brief amount of space. Accordingly, the reader may feel the need to pursue some of the concepts discussed in the chapter in greater detail. To accommodate this potential desire a list of suggested further readings is provided at the end of this section. Even so, a brief overview of what has been discussed in the chapter appears in order.

The chapter began with a brief discussion of the concept of learning outcomes—those observable behaviors that are desired of students after completing a prescribed unit of instruction. The concept of learning outcome was then examined with respect to a procedure called task analysis. It was shown how task analysis could be used to break down a complex learning outcome into its component parts. Of particular interest was the role that task analysis plays in sequencing instruction from basic to more complex behavior.

Attention was then directed to a concern about the basic competencies in a task analysis. This was done by relating task analysis procedures to preassessment. That discussion ultimately centered on a concern about how to define the lowest level of behaviors in a task analysis. It was suggested that a potential dilemma facing many teachers is the practical need to assume certain prerequisite behaviors on the learners' part without formally assessing their ability to demonstrate such competencies. This issue was examined in detail in the second part of the chapter.

The concept of interaction involvement was introduced as an illustration of the kind of prerequisite competency that may be important for teachers of speech communication to assess. Interaction involvement was defined as the extent to which an individual partakes in a social environment. This definition was expanded upon and illustrated. It was indicated that interaction involvement consists of two dimensions—attentiveness and perceptiveness. These concepts were examined as fundamental behaviors necessary for competent interpersonal communication.

After defining and illustrating the concept of interaction involvement, an 18-item paper-and-pencil questionnaire was presented. Methods of scoring and interpretation were discussed so that teachers could employ the questionnaire as an assessment of students' general interaction involvement. It was suggested that such information might be valuable as preassessment data in courses such as interpersonal and small group communication.

The final sections of the chapter were devoted to a discussion of various general and specific behavioral indexes of interaction involvement. First, general behavior patterns such as self-esteem, temperament, and socially appropriate responses were examined in relation to interaction involvement. Second, eye gaze, gesturing, and speech disfluencies were discussed as possible indicators of levels of interaction involvement.

Overall, the major thrust of the chapter was to suggest that teachers should examine certain fundamental prerequisite competencies that are relevant to instructional units to be covered in a course. Often teachers may assume that all or most students are already able to demonstrate fundamental competencies upon entering a course. While this assumption may be valid in many instances, it would be useful to preassess students' competency levels. Such an assessment would provide valuable information about the extent to which students do, in fact, possess necessary, fundamental competencies. Among the ways this information can be used by teachers are the following: specifying instructional objectives, sequencing instructional units, creating instructional experiences, and developing appropriate evaluation procedures.

SUGGESTED READINGS

ALLEN, R. R., and K. BROWN, (eds.). *Developing Communication Competence in Children*. Skokie, Ill.: National Textbook Company, 1976.

This is an excellent source on basic communication competencies. It contains literature reviews on current themes in communication competence as well as original studies that examine various aspects of defining and identifying factors of communication competence.

FLAVELL, J. H. "The development of inferences about others." In T. Mischell (ed.), *Understanding Other Persons*. Oxford: Basic Blackwell, 1974.

This is a thought-provoking article in which a model of interpersonal inference making is presented. It is extremely relevant to any concerns about basic, prerequisite communication competencies. While the model is intended to describe basic competencies that relate to developing communicators, it also has relevance to basic adult competencies.

GAGNÉ, R.M. *The Conditions of Learning* (3rd ed.). New York: Holt, Rinehart & Winston, 1977.

This book provides a detailed examination of task analysis in relation to a theory of learning that assumes a hierarchical relationship among various types of learning outcomes. It is an excellent source for additional information about task analysis, instructional design, and sequencing of instructional strategies.

HAYNES, J. L. *Organizing a Speech: A Programmed Guide.* Englewood Cliffs, N.J.: Prentice-Hall, Inc., 1973; Haynes, J. L. "Improving instruction in speech communication skills through learning hierarchies: An application to organization. *The Speech Teacher,* 1973, *22,* 237–43.

These sources provide an easy to follow, useful application of task analysis procedures to the teaching of message organization. The sources are useful for both illustrations of task analysis and suggestions for teaching organization principles.

KIBLER, R. J., D. J. CEGALA, K. W. WATSON, L. L. BARKER, and D. T. MILES. *Objectives for Instruction and Evaluation* (2nd ed.). Boston: Allyn & Bacon, Inc., 1981.

This book presents an instructional model consisting of instructional objectives, preassessment, instructional procedures, and evaluation. The role of instructional objectives is discussed in relation to the model and other concepts such as criterion-referenced evaluation, mastery learning, needs assessment, and task analysis.

REFERENCES

BASSETT, R. E., N. WHITTINGTON, and A. STATON-SPICER. "The basics in speaking and listening for high school graduates: What should be assessed?" *Communication Education,* 1978, *27,* 293–303.

BERGER, P. L., and T. LUCKMANN. *The Social Construction of Reality.* New York: Doubleday & Co., Inc., 1967.

BLOOM, B.S. (ed.). *Taxonomy of Educational Objectives–The Classification of Educational Goals, Handbook I: Cognitive Domain.* New York: David McKay Co., Inc., 1956.

BLUMER, H. "Psychological import of the human group." In M. Sheriff and M. O. Wilson (eds.), *Group Relations at the Crossroads.* New York: Harper and Row, 1953.

CEGALA, D. J. "Interaction involvement: A necessary dimension of communicative competence." Paper presented at the annual meeting of the Speech Communication Association, Minneapolis, Minn., 1978.

CEGALA, D.J. "Interaction involvement: A cognitive dimension of communicative competence." *Communication Education,* 1981, *30,* 109–121.

CEGALA, D. J., A. ALEXANDER, and S. SOKUVITZ. "An investigation of eye gaze and its relation to selected verbal behavior." *Human Communication Research,* 1979, *5,* 99–108.

CEGALA, D.J., and R. E. BASSETT. "The goals of speech communication instruction: The teacher's perspective." In R. R. Allen and K. L. Brown (eds.), *Developing Communication Competence in Children.* Skokie, Ill.: National Textbook Company, 1976.

CEGALA, D. J., R. J. KIBLER, L. L. BARKER, and D. T. MILES. "Writing behavioral objectives: A programmed article." *The Speech Teacher,* 1972, *21,* 151–68.

COOPERSMITH, S. *The antecedents of Self-Esteem.* San Francisco: W. H. Freeman & Company Publishers, 1967.

DEL POLITO, C. M. "Elementary and secondary education: Act title II regulations." *Spectra,* 1979, *15,* 5.

EYSENCK, H. J. *Dimensions of Personality.* London: Kegan Paul, Trench, Trubner and Co., Ltd., 1947.

EYSENCK, H. J. *Eysenck on Extraversion.* New York: John Wiley & Sons, Inc., 1973.

EYSENCK, H. J., and S. D. G. EYSENCK. *Personality Structure and Measurement.* London: Rutledge & Kegan Paul, 1969.

EXLINE, R. V., and B. J. FEHR. "Applications of semiosis to the study of visual interaction." In A. W. Siegman and S. Feldstein (eds.), *Nonverbal Behavior and Communication.* Hillsdale, N.J.: Lawrence Erlbaum Associates, 1978.

FILMER, P., M. PHILLIPSON, D. SILVERMAN, and D. WALSH. *New Directions in Sociological Theory.* Cambridge, Mass.: M.I.T. Press, 1972.

FLAVELL, J. H. "The development of inferences about others." In T. Mischell (ed.), *Understanding Other Persons.* Oxford: Basil Blackwell, 1974.

FREEDMAN, N. "The analysis of movement behavior during the clinical interview." In A. W. Siegman and B. Pope (eds.), *Studies in Dyadic Communication.* New York: Pergamon Press, Inc., 1972.

GAGNÉ, R. M. *The Conditions of Learning* (3rd ed.). New York: Holt, Rinehart & Winston, 1977.

GAGNÉ, R. M., and L. J. BRIGGS. *Principles of Instructional Design.* New York: Holt, Rinehart & Winston, 1974.

GALASSI, J. P., J. S. DE LO, M. D. GALASSI, and S. BASTIEN. "The college self-expressions scale: A measure of assertiveness." *Behavior Therapy,* 1974, *5,* 165–171.

GOFFMAN, E. *Interaction Ritual: Essays in Face-to-Face Behavior.* Chicago: Aldine Publishing Co., 1967.

HARPER, R. G., A. N. WIENS, and J. D. MATARAZZO. *Nonverbal Communication: The State of the Art.* New York: John Wiley & Sons, Inc., 1978.

HAYNES, J. L. *Organizing a Speech: A Programmed Guide.* Englewood Cliffs, N.J.: Prentice-Hall, Inc., 1973.

KIBLER, R. J., L. L. BARKER, and D. J. CEGALA. "Behavioral objectives and speech communication instruction." *Central States Speech Journal,* 1970a, *21,* 71–80.

KIBLER, R. J., L. L. BARKER, and D. J. CEGALA. "A rationale for using behavioral objectives in speech instruction." *The Speech Teacher,* 1970b, *19,* 245–56.

KIBLER, R. J., L. L. BARKER, and D. T. MILES. *Behavioral Objectives and Instruction.* Boston: Allyn & Bacon, Inc., 1970.

KIBLER, R. J., D. J. CEGALA, L. L. BARKER and D. T. MILES. *Objectives for Instruction and Evaluation.* Boston: Allyn & Bacon, Inc., 1974.

KIBLER, R. J., D. J. CEGALA, K. WATKINS, L. L. BARKER, and D. T. MILES. *Objectives for Instruction and Evaluation* (2nd ed.). Boston: Allyn & Bacon, Inc., 1981.

KRATHWOHL, D. R., B. S. BLOOM, and B. B. MASIA. *Taxonomy of Educational Objectives—The Classification of Educational Goals, Handbook II: Affective Domain.* New York: David McKay Co., Inc., 1964.

MEHAN, H., and H. WOOD. *The Reality of Ethnomethodology.* New York: John Wiley & Sons, Inc., 1975.

NORTON, R. W. "Foundation of a communicator style construct." *Human Communication Research,* 1978, 99–112.

ROBACK, A. A. *The Psychology of Character.* London: Kegan Paul, 1927.

ROSS, M. "The location and definition of cognitive switching styles in the processing of televised newscasts." Doctoral dissertation, The Ohio State University, 1978.

SIMPSON, E. J. "The classification of educational objectives in the psychomotor domain." In *The Psychomotor Domain,* Vol. 3, Washington: Gryphon House, 1972.

WOLPE, J. *The Practice of Behavior Therapy.* New York: Pergamon Press, Inc., 1969.

WOLPE, J., and A. A. LAZARUS. *Behavior Therapy Techniques: A Guide to the Treatment of Neuroses.* New York: Pergamon Press, Inc., 1966.

CHAPTER THREE
THEORETICAL
EXPLORATIONS
A Developmental Perspective
on the Acquisition
of Communication Characteristics

D. Thomas Porter*

The manner in which people acquire communication aptitudes, abilities, attitudes, and behaviors is the general concern of this book and the particular concern of this chapter. It seems everyone has a favorite area in which to study how these characteristics are acquired. A favorite area is the role teacher expectations

*Dr. Porter is Associate Professor, Department of Communication, at Purdue University.

play in the evaluation of communication abilities. We could also consider several nonverbal dimensions in communication aptitude acquisition. Or, we could concentrate on a single communication attitude—communication apprehension. Finally, we might consider communication behavior; for example, classroom interaction.

THE ACQUISITION OF COMMUNICATION CHARACTERISTICS

Communication is a pervasive phenomenon. Communication occurs wherever there are people; it is "difficult to get a handle on it." Its study is correspondingly pervasive. As a consequence, most theory has had to narrow its focus to one part of "the big picture." The purpose of this chapter, however, is to *broaden* the focus. Here we concentrate not upon the classroom, but upon those developmentally relevant factors which affect the learner before, during, and after the classroom encounter. A major premise of this chapter, therefore, is that the classroom context plays a small, albeit important, role in the acquisition of communication aptitudes, abilities, attitudes, and behaviors. As such, one must look beyond the classroom in order to explore these critical questions:

1. *Why* do people acquire certain communication aptitudes, abilities, attitudes, and behaviors?
2. *When* do people acquire certain communication aptitudes, abilities, attitudes, and behaviors?
3. *How* do people acquire communication aptitudes, abilities, attitudes, and behaviors?

In order to answer such broad questions, a frame of reference must be expanded beyond that of the classroom context. Because of the communication field's one-eyed focus on the classroom, it is a natural consequence that these critical questions have yet to be asked, much less answered. It is important to note why the field has failed to address these questions. They represent the essence, the *raison d'etre* for theory and research in communication. As with most occurrences, there are preceding historical events which help explain the field's current preoccupation with the classroom context.

In 1914 a group of "English" teachers met to organize the National Association of Teachers of Public Speaking. For them, secession from traditional academic ranks was a matter of academic freedom. Their academic declaration of independence focused on standards of behavior and excellence developed for the *traditional* English teacher. They wanted to be judged and rewarded according to what they did and did best—teach public speaking. So from the very beginning of the modern development of the communication field, what happened in the classroom was *the* central concern.

As this organization grew from a score of people to over seven thousand, their academic standards and interests grew as well. "How people teach speech" was a central concern for generations. In the 1950s, written communication and in the 1960s, nonverbal communication were added, so "how people teach *communication*" became a central concern. Centrality of concern, however, has not always meant equity in the flailing attempts of the field to justify itself to academe in particular and society in general. In an attempt to avoid low status on the academic totem pole, communication scholars forgot their historical roots, steered away from "pedagogical" concerns, and turned toward theoretical, philosophical, and methodological plundering of other fields whose positions were high on the academic totem pole. For example, Gestalt-oriented theories of communication were plundered from the psychologist who had borrowed the physicist's field theory of atomic structure. The philosophy of the logical-positivist-empiricist was stolen from the social scientist who had borrowed it from the nonscientific mathematician. Experimental design and configurations were lifted from the educational psychologist who had plundered same from the agronomist statistician. And so it went.

In an attempt to exploit the communication field's new-found academic credibility, it lost it. As the Romans plundered other cultures for their wealth, the communication field began to worship the philosophy, theory, and methodology of the social sciences. Of course, the Roman Empire became "wealthy" by plunder. In like manner, communication has benefited from adopting the philosophy of the logical positivist, the theories of the psychologist, and the statistical methods of the agronomist.[1] But academic plunder also contributed new maladies. The field has become justifiably neurotic about the degree to which its plundered "wealth" is appropriate to its central concern—communication. It is difficult, for example, to justify statistical procedures designed for assessing corn seed hybrids to that relationship which exists when people are "communicating." Yet, such procedures are commonly employed without sanction. In short, the field has self-evident notions about communication which are not consistent with the notions plundered from other fields of inquiry.

In 1914 the central concern of communication scholars was to develop techniques to elicit "speaker success." As the years went by, pressure to obtain academic credibility and integrity increased. Unfortunately, the plunder and corresponding idolatry of other field's ideas were used to ease this pressure. For example, the field found itself examining everything from physiological measures of anxiety to eye-blinks as measures of deception. As a result, there became few areas of inquiry that were not "communication" research. There also became few areas of inquiry the field could justifiably call its exclusive domain.

---

[1] The vast majority of traditional statistical techniques were designed originally for static events. For example, analysis of variance was developed to compare various plots of soil by their ability to produce agricultural yields. The "student's *t*" test was developed to compare various methods of brewing beer.

Fortunately, there is at least one area of inquiry which the communication field can justifiably claim as its soverign territory.[2] This claim is found in its historical roots. In 1914 scholars were concerned with how best to elicit communication attributes from the classroom encounter. If one looks to the field's historical heritage, there is a modern birthright to an exclusive domain within the academic enterprise—when, why, and how people acquire communication characteristics. If one fails, however, to explore beyond the classroom context, as did the field's modern forefathers, a one-eyed, narrow perspective results. The basic premise of this chapter, therefore, is that one must go beyond the classroom context in which to find answers to these three critical questions.

In the search for answers one can look back to the Greek philosopher, Heraclitus, who provided a useful perspective as to how human beings do what they do. Heraclitus likened life to a moving river, ever changing, always moving, and never the same. The social and economic ideas of Karl Marx also demonstrated a heavy reliance upon this *developmental* perspective. The clearest example, however, of the contributions and rich theoretical potential that a developmental view can provide is the work of Darwin. Social impacts aside, Darwin's theory of evolution was the first employment of a developmental model to revolutionize thought within an area of inquiry. Its impact on biology was horrific and direct. Its impact on related fields of ethology and primate studies, and on the psychology of Freud, Erickson, and Piaget has been just as profound, although not as direct.

THE DEVELOPMENTAL MODEL

The principal topic of this book is the acquisition of communication aptitudes, abilities, attitudes, and behaviors. There are three major reasons why a developmental perspective is the best perspective by which to address this topic. First,

[2] A field's claim to conceptual territory is a first step to becoming an academic discipline. Formal academic credibility is often associated with the degree to which a given area of inquiry is *disciplinary* in nature. Communication as an area of inquiry is more correctly termed a "field." It does not meet the criteria which are thought to be characteristic of a "discipline." Among these criteria are "congealed" parameters which imply a recognizable set of limits on what constitutes *communication* research and what does not. "Congealed" is purposely used here because a rigid set of parameters would dictate a stagnant area of inquiry, not unlike some "disciplines" to whose academic integrity the communication field often aspires. Finally, it is important to note "failure" to achieve "disciplinary" status is not inherently bad. There are numerous conceptual and sociological advantages for resisting pressures to become more "disciplinary." Among these are the freedoms to generate parameters of study as the need arises, the personal freedom to explore that which interests the scholar, and the freedom to argue for resources (for example, grant monies) as a function of redefined, noncongealed parameters. In short, there are advantages *and* disadvantages for acquiring disciplinary status. "Disciplines" may have an easier time of attracting grant resources because of their scientific status among funding agencies. Yet, phenomena such as communication often do not fall neatly into *one* academic discipline. As a consequence, *multidisciplinary* research is continually plagued by academic chauvinism, isolationism, and territoriality.

the developmental model is isomorphic (that is, conceptually and operationally similar) to a process conceptualization of communication. Second, the inherent nature of the developmental model compels exploration of multiple times and contexts (for example, beyond the classroom context). Third, the developmental model offers heuristic values for communication—that is, it can generate new ideas for theory, research, and practical advancement.

As noted earlier, a field of inquiry often expands its conceptual frontiers by exploiting the advances in philosophy, theory, and methodology made by fields other than its own. Negative side effects can accrue from such plundering when the adopted ideas are not appropriate to their new application. For example, the philosophical stance of the logical positivist suggests that in order for a cause and effect relationship to be tested, "cause" must come *before* "effect." In other words, a teacher must signal "class is over" before the students engage in leave-taking behavior. But in the real world, cause and effect are often not distinguishable from each other; they are often simultaneous. The message, "class is over" may have been the *effect* of the teacher noticing the clock on the wall and *at the same time* be the *cause* of students gathering their books together. Thus, the logical positivist philosophy (and the theory and methodology it generates) is often not appropriate to the study of communication as *process*.

Borrowing ideas from other fields is not necessarily detrimental. Negative side effects happen when borrowed ideas are not appropriate to their new application. In this case, however, the basic ideas of the developmental perspective and a process perspective of communication are virtually synonymous. Therefore, the deployment of the developmental model in communication inquiry may have potentially the same values for communication as it did for biology, ethology, and psychology.

Characteristics of the Communication Process

The basic tenets of a process perspective of communication are fourfold: Communication is (1) dynamic, (2) complex, (3) systemic, and (4) comprised of simultaneous causes and effects. Communication is "dynamic" because of its fluid nature. Messages are always shifting, having different meanings from time to time. For example, consider the following episode. A man thinks he's no longer in love with his wife. He wants out. Symbolically and behaviorally he signals to her, "I hate you." If received by his wife as intended, the "I hate you" message will for the immediate future (if not long term) make their relationship worse. All of the apologies, explanations, denials, or even "But, I really *love* you" messages can never completely compensate for the previous message of despicable hatred. The man can never "uncommunicate" his message of hatred. The wife may "forgive" and "understand"; but, if human, she will never forget. Their communicative relationship may even become stronger or weaker, but it will never be the same. Communication is *dynamic*.

Communication is also "complex." There are a variety of factors which affect the communicative relationship between people. For example, the personality of *an* individual has an almost infinite set of dimensions. When you put two individuals together in a communicative context, you could say, metaphorically at least, there are infinity-squared variables affecting that relationship and its outcomes. Infinity squared is a large number. Communication is *complex.*

Communication is not only dynamic and complex, it is also "systemic." Of all those variables known to affect communication exchanges, most are systemic—that is, they are interdependent, interactional. For example, consider a four year old's first attempt at nonegocentric expression. If one tries to study scientifically those messages, a whole host of potential variables come to mind—chronological age, mental age, gender, intelligence, parental pressures, and so on. Most of these variables are, however, systemic. It would be faulty reasoning to predict "success" in nonegocentric expression from a set of variables like the above without considering their *inter*relationships. Such reasoning could lead one to conclude mental age and intelligence were equally good "predictors" of nonegocentric expression. Yet, a *systemic* investigation would show that mental age and intelligence are so highly related that the effects of other variables are not detectable even though critically important. Communication is *systemic.*

Communication is also comprised of multiple, simultaneous causes and effects. This principle is important to emphasize for two reasons: (1) It characterizes what we know to be *self-evident* about the *process* of communication; (2) There are few, if any, traditional philosophical or methodological means which are able to deal with simultaneous causes and effects. Communication has events which are simultaneously causes and effects. For example, the message, "I hate you," could be the *effect* of a parent's spanking behavior. The "I hate you" message could also be, at the *same* point in time, the *cause* for an "I'm sorry" message from the parent. Communication as *process* does not neatly fit into an "if that, then this" type of thinking. Communication is comprised of *simultaneous causes and effects.*

Characteristics of the
Developmental Model

The developmental perspective's key concept is "development." Not to be confused with a simple linear progression of growth, development is a much more complex model of viewing how things mature. Development is a progression through sequential stages. What occurs at one stage becomes transformed into something that is related to what occurred before, but is also different from what occurred before. Thus, for example, human beings begin life with a genetic and species heritage. Children develop their senses by exploring new ways of communicating hunger, the need for love, and the "me" message. As all of these symbol systems are initially segregated by function, a basic process of development happens—*differentiation.* When all of these symbol systems are used to signal a functional message, the process is called *integration*. Thus the arrangement of *differentiated* symbol systems to achieve a given communicative goal is called *integration*. In short, the key elements used to distinguish the linear process of growth from the process of development are the stages in which components become both *differentiated* and *integrated* at more complex levels of functional usage.

Not only is "development" characterized by *differentiation* and *integration,* it is also *unidirectional.* In other words, what happens at any given time in the process is dependent upon what has happened up to that point in time. There is a relatively stable order of progression. The progression of states goes from simpler to complex. For example, consider the situation where two strangers meet. They initially explore the symbol systems they have in common—"Do you know so-and-so?" "What part of the country are you from?" "What is your sign?" From these simpler exchanges, more complex messages can be exchanged—"You are very attractive." "Do you think I'm a good lover?" "I like country music, do you?" In short, strangers rarely exchange intimate details of their feelings until some relatively simple, base-line symbols have been exchanged.

The fourth and final element of the developmental process is the concept of *event significance.* This element suggests that events have meaning dependent upon *when* those events occur during the developmental process. Thus, the timing of an event in the sequence of events is stressed as an important factor in studying processes. Instructional sequencing is based upon this principle. For example, the introduction of binary number skills into an instructional sequence is successful only when the timing is appropriate; that is, when the child can use the skills and, therefore, improve the probability of retaining them.

When one compares the basic ideas of the developmental model to the basic ideas of a *process* notion of communication, one can see a good deal of conceptual similarity. Communication as process holds communication to be complex. Developmental ideation has the comparable component of *differentiation*— that is, there are a host of variables affecting the developmental process which are segregated by function (purpose). The communication as process notion is conceptualized as systemic—that is, its parts are interdependent, interactional. The developmental perspective has a comparable component—*integration;* simpler variables are *inter*dependently organized so as to form more complex systems. Communication is dynamic. So is the *event significance* dimension of the developmental perspective. Events are important to a given individual *when* they occur in the stream of ongoing development. Finally, communication is comprised of simultaneous causes and effects. The *unidirectionality* of the developmental model incorporates this simultaneity by emphasizing the prediction of events and their simultaneous nature.

The belabored comparison above suggests two implications. First, the adaptation of the developmental perspective to communication should not yield the negative side effects often ascribed to such "borrowing." Second, the adoption of the developmental perspective is appropriate conceptually. The developmental model metaphor provides a frame of reference by which we can explain the full dimensions of why, when, and how people acquire their communication aptitudes, abilities, attitudes, and behaviors.

As noted earlier, the principal topic of this book is how people acquire various communication characteristics. The developmental model was chosen to explore this central concern. The discussion above contrasted the notions of communication as process and development as process. It found the ideas to be conceptually similar. The discussion to follow shows how the inherent nature of the developmental perspective goes beyond a single context in which events are observed.

The inherent nature of the developmental model calls for the exploration of root causes. For example, the typical approach to generating communication competencies has been to concentrate on what the *teacher* and *curriculum* do. Of course, the development of such communication competencies does not begin or end with the classroom. As a function of genetic heritage (for example, basic intelligence) and species heritage (for example, being primates), people are born with certain communication aptitudes. Intelligence is the major primate aptitude which insures our survival. Yet intelligence without a corresponding aptitude to develop and use symbol systems would negate most survival advantages attributed to higher levels of intelligence. In fact, from the time of Saint Augustine (circa 400 A.D.) until today, the development and use of symbol systems has been an index (and at times, a theological "proof") that *Homo sapiens* was in fact superior to primate cohorts.[3] The implication of this thinking is that communication aptitudes cannot and should not be studied in a vacuum. These aptitudes play an important role in what communication competencies can be expected from a given individual. These aptitudes are inherited and nurtured from many other sources than those found in the formal learning structures of the classroom.

A more important implication of the above discussion is that instinctual patterns are important in the discovery of *why* people develop symbol system manipulation capability (that is, communication competencies). These instinctual patterns of behavior are normally overlooked in traditional research when the *classroom* is the contextual focus. Human instincts may not be of the same form as other species, nor would one expect them to be. But the same "urges" to move in a pattern of behaviors which will insure survival and provide primordial, bio-basic fulfillment of needs is present in humans nonetheless. Thus, the study of these instincts should be part and parcel of our efforts to understand *why* people have certain communication aptitudes.

[3] The latest research on this issue of course raises the specter that *Homo sapiens* is not alone in the ability to manipulate true symbol systems. For an excellent discussion of the evolution of these symbols systems, see the work of the British scholar, Peter Marler (Marler & Hamilton 1966). See also Marler (1977) and Burghardt (1977).

The root causes of communication characteristics are found not only in genetic and species heritages, but also in the social ambiance of humans. The particular communication attitudes an individual possesses can be attributed only partially to those events occurring in the classroom. The social nature of human beings is also instinctual. Hamburg (1963) provides this excellent summary:

> . . . primates are group-living forms; the primate group is a powerful adaptive mechanism; emotional processes that facilitate interindividual bonds (participation in group living) have selective advantage; the formation of such bonds is pleasurable for primates; they are easy to learn and hard to forget; their disruption is unpleasant and precipitates profound psychological changes that tend to restore close relations with others of the same species. (p. 305)

It is clear that a proper study of how people acquire certain communication abilities and aptitudes includes the social context in which they learned those abilities and aptitudes. It is also clear that the classroom context is only *one* of many contexts in which these characteristics are acquired.

A major characteristic of human beings is their need for maintaining vital relationships. One such vital relationship is the degree of security found in sibling and parental affiliation. The disruption or abandonment of these affiliative bonds is termed *separation anxiety* (Bowlby 1960, 1969; Averill 1968). The significance of this human factor cannot be overstated. When one communication attitude, communication apprehension (Porter 1977), is examined in the classroom, there may be a significant oversight if this primordial phenomenon of separation anxiety is ignored. On the assumption that some communication apprehension accrues from negative classroom interactions in the primary grades, the more basic question is left unanswered: To what degree is separation anxiety contributing to an individual's communication apprehension, fears, and anxieties? It is a reasonable conjecture that the separation from comfortable communication relationships (friends, parents, or siblings) may be the root *cause* of communication apprehension. This hypothesis has particular relevance, of course, when the classroom by definition separates an individual from normal communicative relationships. The classroom context is intentionally synthetic. Why would we not expect people to fear communicative settings where naturally occurring social supports are purposely eliminated? In short, the developmental model promotes exploration *beyond* the classroom context as to why people have certain communication attitudes (in this case, communication apprehension). Thus, the proper study of when people develop communication attitudes may be the study of *event significance*—that is, the study of events depending on when they occur during development, not when it is convenient to study them in a classroom situation. For example, the significance of communication apprehension in one's communication repertoire may be ascertained by exploring *when* the first disruption of a vital communicative relationship occurred, and not after years of educational manipulation of that repertoire.

It should be fairly clear by the preceding discussions that a developmental perspective and the process perspective of communication "dovetail" conceptually. But the real value of the developmental model lies not in its inherent capability to stretch one's thinking beyond traditional conceptual frontiers, nor in its conceptual similarity to a process view of communication. The true test of any conceptual scheme is the degree to which it generates new thought, theory, and research possibilities—the extent to which it explores *new* conceptual frontiers. It is here that the developmental model displays its heuristic prowess. The adaptation and adoption of a developmental perspective can open to the field of communication a wholly new conceptual frontier to map, explore, and conquer. Ironically, it has been our academic birthright from the modern beginning of the field. To the extent that these frontiers are developed by future generations of communication scholars, the ultimate test of whether the developmental perspective is in fact a useful conceptual scheme will be given. The remainder of this chapter is devoted to exploring some of these conceptual frontiers.

EXPLORATIONS VIA THE DEVELOPMENTAL MODEL

There are a plethora of topics with which the communication scholar could be concerned. None is more central, more uniquely its own, or more critical than the manner in which individuals acquire communication abilities, aptitudes, attitudes, and behaviors. It is to this central domain that the developmental perspective is most applicable. A review of the major facets of the developmental perspective suggest four concepts: *differentiation, integration, unidirectionality,* and *event significance.* Each concept has special implications for exploring the central and unique domain of the communication field.

Differentiation

Differentiation when applied to the development of communication characteristics is their segregation by function or purpose. In other words, a differentiated approach to a complete list of communication characteristics requires a correspondent list of those characteristics' functions. There are a variety of scientific and practical values to such a differentiated approach.

The scientific value of the functional isolation of a given communication characteristic forces one to examine *causes* of that characteristic. Without such an emphasis, one is limited to the stagnant position of simply examining what other characteristics are associated with the characteristic in question. For example, communication is the "tie that binds" social structures together. The family is one such social structure. Because we are reinforced from the very beginning of our existence to "understand" messages from others, there is a good deal of pressure to communicate "we understand" when we actually do not.

Consider this interaction between parent and child. "Now, the reason why you don't want to mention grandmother's fat is that you will hurt her feelings, okay?" The child dutifully responds, "Okay." Of course, anyone in their right mind can see that grandmother is indeed fat, so why can't the child talk about it? Well, the child learns quite early to feign understanding because if he or she does not, significant negative reinforcement will be scheduled—for example, a "look" from the parent that could "kill." So there are communication aptitudes which are reinforced for the function they serve. This particular aptitude, of course, is not limited to children. Adults continually provide feedback that they "understand." To indicate otherwise might result in the continuance of a boring conversational topic, or might demonstrate ignorance about the topic, display lower social status, or even invite retribution from the message sender.

The impact of this differentiated analysis is that it calls for a functional analysis of communication characteristics. Such an analysis provides new avenues for research. In the situation above, the new perspective is not focused exclusively on what is said, but on the *purposes* of "false feedback" so common in human interaction.

One can also find practical value in a differentiated approach to the understanding of communication. One aspect of communication is communication sensitivity. Most human beings are reinforced for their ability to state accurately their feelings, provided there are social supports for such frankness. A differentiated philosophy in one's relations with other people should stimulate a more communicatively sensitive emotional set. For example, consider again the "I hate you" message. Our primordial instinct is to respond in kind with a "I don't particularly care for you, either" message. But, our humanity is at its peak when we attempt to understand the function of the "I hate you" message. The "I hate you" message may come from frustration, a need for affiliation, separation anxiety, or from simple boredom with the relationship. Making hate and making love are equally great stimulants for increasing the intensity of a relationship. In any event, we rise above our primate heritage when we counter the "I hate you" message with a message of "Hey, let's talk about it." In short, the practical utility of exploring the *functional* aspects of messages we receive from others is that we can discover *why* those messages were sent.

Integration

The second major concept of the developmental model is its process of *integration*. Integration is the arrangement of simpler components to form a more complex system. Cells form organs, and organs are organized into bodily systems to provide life. When this metaphor is applied to communication, integration becomes the manner by which an individual combines symbol systems to signal a purposeful message. As with the concept of differentiation, the application of the integration concept has a variety of scientific and practical values to offer the study of communication.

A major scientific value of an *integrated* perspective on communication concerns the academic domain of "relational communication." This study—concerned with the role communication plays in the development of human relationships—can benefit from an integrated approach. In the developmental sense, integration implies the passage from simple to more complex states of human intimacy. As the effects of "future shock" become more intense from the pressures of a highly dynamic society, the reasons why certain relationships are maintained and others dissolved become major issues for communication scholars. Only a study of the social intercourse which initiates, maintains, and dissolves relationships can provide answers to such vexing questions. The developmental model places such issues at the forefront of our conceptual boundaries of theory and research.

If one were to adapt an integrated philosophy to commonplace communication activities, a practical value of the developmental perspective would be detected. Consider, for example, the context in which a teacher and student must resolve a conflict about a final grade. The student recognizes that the ultimate decision lies in the hands of the teacher. The teacher, on the other hand, probably is uncomfortable about making such decisions, particularly if the final grade will cause the student to drop out of school. If both teacher and student were to take an *integrated* approach to this situation, they would recognize that their symbol systems must agree on a simple level before the more complex stage of conflict resolution can occur. In other words, the student should not argue for a higher grade by a "But, I *need* a higher grade" message. Nor should the teacher argue for the current grade by a "Well, that's the grade you've earned" message. Note that both messages may very well be valid. But they do not correspond; they are not integrated by function. The teacher and student must find a common ground (isomorphic symbol systems) in order to resolve the conflict. An integrated philosophy calls for the development of complementary, simple symbol systems before tackling more complex ones.

Unidirectionality

The third major concept of the developmental model is *unidirectionality*. The principle of unidirectionality dictates that events are predicated on and are affected by what has happened before. There is a stable order of progression from simple to complex stages. In other words, what happens at any given point in time of a process is dependent upon what has happened up to that point in time. As one examines the communication phenomenon as process, the degree of scientific and practical value of unidirectionality becomes evident.

For example, consider the attention paid to the roles various communication "traits" play in the acquisition of communication characteristics. No one would reasonably suggest, for example, that communication apprehension be studied as if it had no history, no reason for its degree of existence. It exists, it affects communication behavior, and, therefore, it must be studied. A more sensitive and scientifically justifiable approach to its study, however, would be to quit viewing it as an independent trait. Communication apprehension is derived from (and therefore changed by) previous communicatively salient factors whose historical roots may be years in length. It is those factors which are the proper study for communication apprehension. The developmental model and its perspective of unidirectionality dictate that those factors are indeed the ones where we as a field should concentrate our resources.

The developmental perspective also has much to say about the recent concerns with "communication competency." Communication competency is normally characterized by a triadic set of features: (1) one's repertoire of communication skills, (2) one's ability to select situationally appropriate skills from that repertoire, and (3) one's ability to implement the selected skill. Unfortunately, "communication competency," as popularly conceived, is directly contradictory to self-evident notions about communication. The concept of unidirectionality from the developmental model and the process notion of communication directly contradict such a simplistic notion of communication competence. The competence of a given individual to communicate is not a single idea event; that is, a true photograph of communication competence is developed only from examining the competence of both entities involved. In other words and practically speaking, communication competence is a function of at least two entities, two interactants. One does not "communicate" in a vacuum. If consistently applied, the developmental model prevents such sloppy thinking.

Event Significance

The fourth and final major concept of the developmental model is *event significance*. This concept dictates that events have meaning dependent upon *when* those events occur during the developmental process. The concept of event significance has more to offer the study of communication than perhaps any other feature of the developmental model.

If the significance of events and the point at which they occur in a process were to become a major feature of research and thinking, true explanatory theories could be derived. Without primordial theories as to why, when, and how people acquire communication abilities, aptitudes, attitudes, and behaviors, the communication field will continue to chase speculative hunches about its central and unique domain of inquiry.

Consider, for example, the typical "scientific" study in communication. A couple of variables are measured by questionnaires or behavioral observation and found to be predictive of a couple of indexes of communication effectiveness. The author concludes, "It appears that variable X and variable Y affect communication effectiveness variable Z." The vita of the author is increased by a couple of typewritten lines, the dean is pleased, and the journal article is put on the shelf. What about the reader? A dry taste is left in the mouth. Why? It is reasonable to conclude that communication is much more dynamic than variables X and Y, and there is certainly more to communication effectiveness than variable Z. What is absent in the vast majority of our research on why, when, and how people acquire their communication characteristics is the self-evident component of development. For example, consider again the investigation of communication apprehension. When is the field going to devote the intellectual and monetary resources necessary to isolate the developmental *causes* of people's fear of communication, their unwillingness to communicate? Without such efforts, we will continue to view communication apprehension and similar variables as existing in a black hole, in an intellectual vacuum. Without longitudinal research over a period of years, if not a lifetime, we will never truly identify the causes and effects of communication apprehension. The implementation of a developmental perspective would not allow us to do otherwise.

Consider also the major concern of education—the manipulation of learners' minds and behaviors in order to meet society's and the learner's needs. Given that communication is the most central element in the learning process, why are the effects of our efforts in manipulating those communication characteristics exclusively limited to the classroom? A developmental model dictates that events are significant *when* they occur in a person's "life stream." The proper study, therefore, of the acquisition of communication characteristics is the timing of those events in the process of becoming a truly human being—one who can share symbol systems with other human beings and thereby fulfill the destiny of a nonprimate heritage.

SUMMARY

There are a variety of contexts in which to study how communication characteristics are acquired. The classroom is an important context, but it is only one of many. The study of *other* contexts allows us to consider and systematically study the why, when, and how of people's acquisition of communication aptitudes, abilities, attitudes and behaviors.

The study of communication is difficult. Historically, the communication field has concentrated upon the classroom. Because there is more to life than the classroom, this chapter called for a new model for viewing the acquisition of communicative characteristics. The developmental model was chosen for its inherent compatibility with a *process* notion of communication.

The developmental perspective is concerned with progression through sequential stages. What occurs at one stage becomes transformed into something that is related to what happened before, but is also different from what happened before. Communication is also a series of progressive stages, continually in motion, and dependent on what happened previously.

The process notion of communication has four basic ideas to offer. (1) Communication is dynamic. It is ever changing, always moving, never the same. (2) Communication is systemic. Its parts are interrelated; when one part of the communication system is affected, all parts are affected. (3) Communication is complex. There are a plethora of variables which affect the process of communication and its outcomes. (4) Communication is comprised of simultaneous causes and effects. The *effect* of a previous behavior can *simultaneously* serve as the *cause* for the next sequence of behavior.

The developmental perspective, too, has four basic ideas to consider. (1) Components of a process are differentiated by function. People develop signals and symbols to achieve certain communicative purposes. (2) When these components are *integrated,* they serve to fulfill a need for the person involved. (3) The process is *unidirectional.* It is always moving, ever changing, and continually building upon itself. (4) Events are significant *when* they occur in a stream of activity.

When we compare these two sets of ideas, there is an interesting similarity. This similarity allows the application of the developmental perspective to the study of why, when, and how people acquire their communication aptitudes, abilities, attitudes, and behaviors. This application offers three advantages. (1) Unlike borrowing certain ideas from other fields, a process notion of communication and a developmental perspective are harmonious in ideas and pragmatic application. (2) Multiple contexts and times are the focus rather than a single context or time. (3) New ideas contributing to the exploration of new conceptual frontiers are offered.

By employing the developmental model in the study of why, when, and how people acquire their communication characteristics, numerous scientific and pragmatic advancements can be made. The application of "differentiation" demonstrated the need to study social pressures regarding the "I understand" message. Pragmatically, communication sensitivity was shown to be enhanced by a *differentiated* perspective. The application of "integration" showed the need for studying the changes in a communication relationship as it goes from simple to more complex events. Pragmatically, the resolution of conflict was shown to be superior from an *integrated* perspective. The application of the "unidirectionality" concept displayed the current weakness of studies on communication "traits." Pragmatically, we noted that popular notions of "communication competence" are faulty when *unidirectionality* is used as a perceptual framework. Finally, *event significance* displayed the intellectual stagnancy of many "scientific" studies of communication. Pragmatic implications were also drawn for the examination of communication characteristics via longitudinal research.

REFERENCES

AVERILL, J. "Grief: Its nature and significance." *Psychological Bulletin,* 1968, *70,* 721–28.

BOWLBY, J. *Attachment and Loss, Volume I: Attachment.* New York: Basic Books, Inc., Publishers, 1969.

BOWLBY, J. "Separation anxiety." *International Journal of Psychoanalysis,* 1960, *41,* 83–113.

BURGHARDT, G. M. "Ontogeny of communication." In T. A. Sebeok (ed.), *How Animals Communicate.* Bloomington, Ind.: Indiana University Press, 1977, 71–97.

HAMBURG, D. A. "Emotions in the perspective of human evolution." In P. H. Knapp (ed.), *Expression of the Emotions in Man.* New York: International Universities Press, 1963, 300–317.

MARLER, P. "The evolution of communication." In T. A. Sebeok (ed.), *How Animals Communicate.* Bloomington, Ind.: Indiana University Press, 1977, 45–70.

MARLER, P., and W. J. HAMILTON, III. *Mechanisms of Animal Behavior.* New York: John Wiley & Sons, Inc., 1966.

PORTER, D. T. "Communication apprehension: Communication's latest artifact?" In D. Nimmo (ed.), *Communication Yearbook III.* New Brunswick, N.J.: Transaction Press, 1977.

CHAPTER FOUR
CLASSROOM INTERACTION

Gustav W. Friedrich*

*Dr. Friedrich is Professor and Chairperson, Department of Communication, at the University of Oklahoma.

THE IMPORTANCE OF STUDYING
CLASSROOM INTERACTION

Phillip Jackson observes that, "Aside from sleeping, and perhaps playing, there is no other activity that occupies as much of the child's time as that involved in attending school" (1968, p. 5). Translating Jackson's observation into more concrete terms, each student spends about twelve hundred hours in school each year. Since individuals in the United States—as well as in most developed countries—spend between ten and sixteen years in school, a total of between twelve and twenty thousand hours are spent in the classroom. This significant expenditure of time warrants asking: What is the nature of the interaction that occurs in the classroom?

In reviewing the research related to this question, this chapter will focus its attention on classroom teaching. This mode of instruction, the norm since the end of the nineteenth century when it replaced the country-school practices of individual recitation and peer teaching, consists of a single teacher and a group of twenty to forty students of approximately equal age housed in a rectangular room containing a desk for the teacher and small desks for each student, surrounded by windows, chalkboards, and bulletin boards, and with tile or wood floors. Given projections of declining enrollments and the current political climate for school finances, radical changes in this mode of instruction cannot be expected. With a forecasted 19 percent national decline in the number of eighteen year olds between 1980 and 1990, the prospects for new classrooms are slight. Thus, despite the fact that over 50 percent of all schools built from 1967 to 1970 were open-space schools (generally characterized by a lack of interior walls and by the existence of instructional areas ranging in size from two ordinary classrooms to over thirty), most instruction is likely to continue to occur within the context of a classroom in the traditional "egg crate" school building. The current average of approximately thirty students per classroom is also unlikely to change because, as Berliner and Gage report, decreasing average class size in the state of California by one student would cost $100 million, while a two student decrease would cost $200 million, and a three student decrease $450 million (1976, p. 19). It appears likely, then, that classroom teaching will continue to be the most common form of instruction.

APPROACHES TO STUDYING
CLASSROOM INTERACTION

What, then, do we know about this form of instruction? Research studies designed to shed light on this question have been appearing in the literature since the year 1896. With considerable overlap, such studies are the product of four paradigms of research.

1. *Trait-rating paradigm.* The earliest attempts used students as observers. Kratz (1896), for example, asked large numbers of students to describe the "best" teachers they ever had and subjected the list to a form of content analysis which yielded lists of characteristics of "good" teachers. Beginning about 1917, researchers began to ask these questions of experts—school administrators, professors of education, and others—whose opinions were presumed to have greater validity than those of students. A popular, related approach consisted of examining rating scales used for teacher evaluation in an attempt to locate elements considered important enough to rate.

2. *Trait-observation paradigm.* Dissatisfaction with using someone's opinion as a criterion measure of teacher effectiveness came early. The empirical basis for this dissatisfaction was provided by Barr and others as early as 1935 when they demonstrated that correlations between ratings of teachers and mean pupil gains on achievement tests were quite low (ranging from $-.15$ to $+.36$, with a mean of $+.16$). The methodology for early systematic observation studies came largely from the Child Study Movement of the 1920s. Because they were studying children too young to be tested or interviewed and because the most convenient place to work with such children was the classroom, these researchers pioneered the use of direct observation of classroom behaviors. The earliest study using this approach (attempting to describe what a teacher does rather than how well he or she does it) was Stevens's (1912) excellent study of questioning behavior—a study which will be described later in this chapter. While a number of developments prevented this movement from becoming immediately popular (Medley 1972), in 1954 Barr was able to devote an entire issue of the *Journal of Experimental Education* to a review of seventy-five relevant studies done in Wisconsin under his direction.

3. *Structure paradigm.* Scholars in the late forties began to focus their attention on ways of structuring the classroom environment in such a fashion as to minimize the impact of teacher differences and maximize student learning. Discussion was compared with lecturing; programmed instruction with simulation and games.

4. *Process-product paradigm.* Predictably, in retrospect, because it ignored the complexity and dynamics of the classroom environment, a great deal of research failed to discover one approach superior to others for any grade level. Dubin and Traveggia, for example, after reviewing ninety-one studies, suggest: "These data demonstrate clearly and unequivocally that there is no measurable difference among truly distinctive methods of college instruction when evaluated by student performance on final examination" (1968, p. 23). As such evidence continued to accumulate, researchers in the sixties began to isolate and examine elements of teaching behavior which could be used to compare various method-

ologies (for example, level of question asking is a variable appropriate to both discussion and programmed instruction)—isolating well over one thousand such variables. Such an approach produced an explosion of both descriptive and experimental systematic observation research which centered on identifying linkages between instructional strategies (processes) and learning outcomes (products). An exploration of the status of this body of research forms the core of this chapter. Narrowing the focus of the chapter in this fashion requires two caveats. First, the process-product paradigm is largely the province of educational psychologists rather than that of communication researchers. The goal of the chapter, therefore, is not to summarize what we know about classroom interaction. The chapter is instead intended as an exploration of what we can learn about classroom interaction when viewed through the lens of the process-product paradigm. The second caveat stems from the first. Scholars from a wide variety of disciplines, including speech communication, are heavily involved in exploring the dynamics of classroom communication. The reader of the chapter, therefore, needs to remember that while the process-product paradigm is currently one of the major approaches to studying classroom interaction, it is neither the only approach nor is it necessarily the most valuable approach to doing research in the area.

DESCRIPTIVE INFORMATION
ON CLASSROOM INTERACTION

Activities of the Classroom

What, then, have we learned from research within the process-product paradigm? Nuthall and Snook (1973) summarize numerous studies which suggest that the instructional activities of a classroom can be categorized in three basic forms.

1. *Individual Work*—the student is working on his or her own. Individual work accounts for between 25 and 45 percent of all class time.
2. *Extended Discourse*—the teacher is talking, performing, demonstrating, or exhibiting materials. Extended discourse accounts for between 18 and 22 percent of all class time.
3. *Interactive Discourse*—the teacher and students are talking with each other. The degree of teacher control varies. Interactive discourse accounts for between 34 and 53 percent of all class time.

Moves in Interactive Discourse

In focusing their attention on interactive discourse in the classroom, Arno Bellack (1966) and his colleagues at Teachers College, Columbia University, describe a language "game" with rules for both teacher and student players. Four "moves" allow players to achieve the object of the game which is to engage in verbal discourse about subject matter (p. 4).

1. *Structuring.* Structuring moves serve the pedagogical function of setting the context for subsequent behavior by either launching or halting-excluding interaction between students and teachers. For example, teachers frequently launch a class period with a structuring move in which they focus attention on the topic or problem to be discussed during that session.
2. *Soliciting.* Moves in this category seek to elicit a verbal response, to encourage persons addressed to attend to something, or to elicit a physical response. All questions are solicitations, as are commands, imperatives, and requests.
3. *Responding.* These moves bear a reciprocal relationship to soliciting moves and occur only in relation to them. Their pedagogical function is to fulfill the expectation of soliciting moves; thus, students' answers to teachers' questions are classified as responding moves.
4. *Reacting.* These moves are occasioned by a structuring, soliciting, responding, or prior reacting move, but are not directly elicited by them. Pedagogically, these moves serve to modify (by clarifying, synthesizing, or explaining) and/or to rate (positively or negatively) what has been said previously. Reacting moves differ from responding moves; while a responding move is always directly elicited by a solicitation, preceding moves serve only as the occasion for reactions. Rating by a teacher of a student's response, for example, is designated as a reacting move.

The rules stipulate that the teacher must do most of the talking (approximately two-thirds) and must structure the specific form and content of the verbal game. Played according to the rules, the teacher will spend most of the time asking questions and commenting on student responses, although, from time to time, he or she will spend time structuring the content and providing summaries of previous discourse.

The rules for students are more restrictive. Their primary task is to answer questions—to reply when called on. At all times the student must respond as though the teacher is asking only questions a student should be able to answer. While each student will be expected to respond no more than six or seven times in an hour, he or she is expected to pay attention to the progress of the lesson. After the student has responded, the response will be repeated, praised, or otherwise commented on by the teacher. In short, most of the student's time will be taken up listening to other students' responses and the teacher's comments on those responses.

Stability of Classroom Interaction

It is interesting to note that this classroom language game has not changed substantially in seventy years (Hoetker & Ahlbrand 1969). The earliest major systematic study of classroom interaction cited is a report by Romiett Stevens in

1912 on her four years of observing classrooms. Her results virtually duplicate those of Bellack. She found that, on the average, teachers talked 64 percent of the time—there was little difference between teachers in this regard no matter what the subject or grade level—about 80 percent of the classroom talk was devoted to asking, answering, or reacting to questions; and the rate of teacher question asking ranged from one to four questions per minute, with the average being about two per minute.

Adding additional support to Hoetker and Ahlbrand's conclusion is a study by Meredith D. Gall (1970) of the use of questions in teaching.

> It is reasonable to conclude that in a half-century there has been no essential change in the types of questions which teachers emphasize in the classroom. About 60 percent of teachers' questions require students to recall facts; about 20 percent require students to think; and the remaining 20 percent are procedural. (p. 713)

Research summarized by Raymond Adams (1972) indicates that these results are not unique to the United States. Dahllof and Lundgren (1970), for example, discerned "amazing" similarities in patterns between American and Swedish data in terms of the amount of "teacher structuring" (91 percent and 86 percent), "soliciting" (81 percent and 86 percent), "responding" (22 percent and 12 percent), and "reacting" (16 percent and 21 percent). Similar results are available for Australia, New Zealand, and Great Britain.

PRESCRIPTIVE INFORMATION
ON CLASSROOM INTERACTION

Lack of Empirical Support

Given a model of teaching that has endured for so long, one would assume the existence of a wealth of empirical evidence supporting the model. Such, however, is not the case. After reviewing the available literature, Heath and Nielson (1974) report.

> Our analysis of this literature leads us to [these] conclusions: First, the research literature on the relation between teacher behavior and student achievement does not offer an empirical basis for the prescription of teacher-training objectives. Second, this literature fails to provide such a basis, not because of minor flaws in statistical analyses, but because of sterile operational definitions of both teaching and achievement, and because of fundamentally weak research designs. (p. 481)

Gage reminds us that "such discouraging characterizations of previous findings go back at least 25 years (see, for example, Committee on the Criteria for

Teacher Effectiveness, 1952) and are still being repeated in present-day publications" (1978, p. 24). To illustrate, Doyle, after examining nine reviews, asserted in 1977: "Reviewers have concluded, with remarkable regularity, that few consistent relationships between teacher variables and effectiveness criteria can be established" (p. 164).

Available Alternatives

The situation, then, is this: For seventy years, teachers have interacted with their students using a relatively consistent pattern. Yet, after thousands of research studies, we are unable to say that those interactions have any significant impact on learning. How are we to respond to this state of affairs? Four of the more common reactions, following the analysis of Dunkin and Biddle (1974), can be summarized in terms of the following "philosophies" of teaching:

1. Teaching as Creed
2. Teaching as Art
3. Teaching as Ineffective
4. Teaching as Problem-Solving

Teaching as creed.   From the practitioner's perspective, the most common response has been that of teaching as creed. With no research to support choice, Wallen and Travers (1963) suggest that creeds are

1. Derived from teaching traditions (for example, we teach as we were taught)
2. Derived from social learnings in our background (for example, we reinforce the behavior of pupils so as to develop a middle-class ideology)
3. Derived from philosophical traditions (for example, we teach in accordance with the Rogerian or the Skinnerian tradition)
4. Generated by our own needs (for example, we adopt a lecture method because we need to be self-assertive)
5. Generated by conditions existing in the school or community (for example, we conduct our classroom in such a way as to produce formal and highly disciplined behavior because this represents the pattern required by the principal)

Whether teachers would base their choice on research evidence were it available is an open question. Clifford suggests that they might not, basing her argument on "the poor understanding of research in professional populations, the tiny proportions of teachers or administrators in research organizations, the reports that under one-half of a large sample of teachers read even one professional book a year, and the fact that administrators rated research publications least useful as a source of knowledge" (1973, p. 22). She concludes: "It is arguable that research survived less for its substantive support of educational practice or innovation than simply as an activity *expected* of an expert group" (1973, p. 28). Whatever the case, creeds must currently be justified on the basis of enthusiasm and/or plausible argument rather than on empirical data. It is possible, therefore, to move from television as creed in the 1950s to teaching machines and programmed instruction in the 1960s to mastery learning and performance or competency-criteria in the 1970s. While not rejecting any of these instructional strategies as useful options, it is necessary to point out that there is not now, and there will not be for some time, any empirical evidence on which to base choices among them. Thus, choice among alternative creeds remains haphazard and, at best, must be based on a combination of logic, clinical insight, raw experience, and common sense. In such a situation, as Gage observes, education is "more than ever at the mercy of powerful and passionate writers who shift educational thinking ever more erratically with their manifestos" (1978, p. 41).

Teaching as art. A more sophisticated response consists of arguing that teaching is an art in the dictionary sense of "a specific skill in adept performance, conceived as requiring the exercise of intuitive facilities that cannot be learned solely by study" (*American Heritage,* 1969). From this perspective, it is both foolish and impossible to attempt to discover laws that connect classroom communication with learning—they simply do not exist. As Gilbert Highet argues

> It seems to me very dangerous to apply the aims and methods of science to human beings as individuals. . . . Teaching involves emotions, which cannot be systematically appraised and employed, and human values, which are quite outside the grasp of science. . . . "Scientific" teaching, even of scientific subjects, will be inadequate as long as both teachers and pupils are human beings. Teaching is not like inducing a chemical reaction: it is much more like painting a picture or making a piece of music, or on a lower level, like planting a garden or writing a friendly letter. (1954, pp. vii–viii)

While this position possesses some plausibility, N. L. Gage makes the important point that

> Painting and composing, and even friendly letter-writing and casual conversation, have inherent order and lawfulness that can be subjected to theoretical analysis. . . . The artist whose lawfulnesses are revealed does not become an automaton; ample scope remains for his subtlety and individuality. . . .
> So it is with teaching. Although teaching requires artistry, it can be subjected to scientific scrutiny. The power to explain, predict, and control that may result from such scrutiny will not dehumanize teaching. (1964, pp. 270–71)

James Gallagher makes the point even more strongly when he observes

> Is teaching an art? Indeed it is. Perhaps too much of one. Surgery was once too much an art and many people died as a result. Cooking is an art,

and while few people die of it these days, drugstores do a thriving business in remedies for misbegotten creative culinary efforts. For when a set of skills is in a developmental stage where people say "It is an art," they mean several things. First, that there are only a very few persons who have the skills that can identify them as highly effective practitioners, as "artists." Second, even these artists cannot give a systematic account of how they practice their art, and they are reduced to modeling their performance for those who would learn from them. But it is hard to imitate the true artist, and his genius too often dies with him. . . .

Those interested in the improvement of education and teaching would like to remove some of the mystery of the art of effective teaching through systematic study. (1970, p. 30)

Teaching as ineffective. A third reaction is to argue that teaching plays a very minor role in learning and, therefore, one should not expect to find significant relationships between classroom communication and learning. The Coleman report (1966) and its offshoots (Jencks 1972; Mosteller & Moynihan 1972) have frequently been used to argue this position. Such individuals claim that family background, socioeconomic status, ethnicity, and the like are the major causal variables that affect differences in achievement, between schools, and that teachers only minimally affect student achievement. Heath and Nielson (1974), cited earlier, reached the same conclusion in their review of the studies of teacher clarity, use of student ideas, criticism, enthusiasm, and other variables commonly accepted as skills or competencies. They concluded, first, that there is no established empirical relation between teacher behavior and student achievement; second, that the flaws in the research are due to nonsensical statistical analyses, weak research designs, and sterile operational definitions of teacher behavior and student outcomes; and third, because of the strong association between omnibus measures of student achievement and socioeconomic and ethnic status, the effects of teachers and techniques of teaching on achievement are bound to be trivial.

A MODEL OF CLASSROOM LEARNING

While it is difficult to argue with Heath and Nielson's first two points, whether or not they are correct about socioeconomic and ethnic influences is still an open question. Dunkin and Biddle (1974), for example, make the point that the studies which support this argument are "statistically artifactive and are based on differences among schools rather than among individual teachers or classrooms" (p. 20). To develop the argument in a more positive fashion, a theory of classroom learning will be explicated. While the terminology and order of presentation have been changed, the ideas and the data supporting them are drawn largely from Benjamin S. Bloom's (1976) book *Human Characteristics and School Learning.* Three independent variables are central to the theory:

1. *Student ability:* The extent to which the student already possesses the basic prerequisites for instruction
2. *Student motivation:* The extent to which the student is (or can be) motivated to engage in the learning process
3. *Quality of classroom communication:* The utility of teacher-student and student-student interactions for learning

The outcomes, or dependent variables, that are a product of these three independent variables and their interactions are *level and type of achievement*— that is, the degree to which the student acquires specified knowledge, skills and/ or attitudes. Because the research is more thoroughly developed in the area of knowledge, this review is focused primarily on knowledge as the dependent variable.

Student Ability

Specifying the independent impact of student ability on the learning of content can be done at both the macro- (over a total course of instruction) and micro- (over a unit of instruction within a course) level. At the macrolevel, student abilities can be assessed by achievement tests (actual learning of content), aptitude tests (ability to learn content), and general intelligence tests (a global measure of aptitude). Summarizing Bloom's data for these four sources of prediction, we discover that

1. *Achievement tests:* In general, almost three-fourths of the variation in achievement at the end of the course is predictable from a measure of achievement or pretest before the course started.
2. *Aptitude tests:* For introductory courses in arithmetic, mathematics, reading, and a second language, the relation between total scores on aptitude measures and later achievement in these courses (either grades or achievement tests) averages about .63 (.70 when corrected for the unreliability of the measure).
3. *General intelligence measures:* Typically correlate about .50 ($\pm$ .10) with achievement over a great variety of courses and subjects.
4. *Unit tests:* In microstudies of mastery learning conducted at the University of Chicago, student ability accounted for about 50 percent of the variation in achievement.

Based on four sources of prediction, therefore, it seems safe to conclude that student ability can account for up to one-half ($r = .70$) of the variance on relevant cognitive achievement measures.

Student Motivation

Student motivation refers to the fact that individuals vary in what they are emotionally prepared to learn as expressed in their interests, attitudes, and self-views. Like student abilities, motivation has been measured at both the macro-

and microlevel. At the macrolevel, measurement has focused on subject-related affect, school-related affect, and academic self-concept. Summarizing Bloom's data we discover

1. *Subject-related affect:* International Study of Achievement (IEA) studies in mathematics, science, literature, reading comprehension, French as a second language, and English as a second language discovered that affect toward a subject generally accounts for between 10 and 17 percent of the variation in achievement—with a few studies, especially in the later years of school, reaching almost 20 percent of the variation in achievement.
2. *School-related affect:* Attitudes toward school and school learning can account for as much as 20 percent of the variation in school achievement. The correlation is relatively low in grades 1–5 but grows stronger with age.
3. *Academic self-concept:* Attitudes toward self in regard to school learning account for about 25 percent of the variation in school achievement after the elementary school period. The relationship is lower for academic self-concept in a particular subject (math, science) than it is for general academic self-concept. Combining two or three of the measures listed so far to predict school achievement yields no higher relation than the highest of the two or three. For prediction purposes, therefore, academic self-concept is the most useful.
4. *Unit interest:* In general, interest at the beginning of a learning task and achievement at the end of the task correlate about .30 (.38). The relation between achievement at the end of one learning task and interest at the beginning of the next learning task averages about .30 (.38) also. Thus achievement and subject-matter affect are interrelated and each influences the other in a kind of spiral effect.

Based on four sources of prediction, therefore, it seems safe to conclude that student motivation can account for up to one-fourth (r = .50) of the variance on relevant cognitive achievement measures.

Independently, then, student ability allows us to account for 50 percent of achievement and student motivation for 25 percent. When we combine the two variables in a prediction equation, because they are correlated we are able to account for 65 percent of the variance on relevant cognitive achievement measures. That is, 65 percent of the learning that occurs in a classroom is determined by prior student ability and student motivation. The remaining 35 percent must be partitioned among quality of classroom interaction, measurement error, and a variety of other potentially relevant variables.

Quality of Classroom Communication

Classroom communication is not a product of teacher characteristics—they rarely account for more than 5 percent of the achievement variation of students. Neither is it a product of characteristics of classrooms and schools—these characteristics rarely yield correlations which account for more than 5 percent of achievement variation. It is teaching, not the teacher, and classroom environment, not physical characteristics, that influence school learning. Bloom's review of relevant literature suggests that the effects of *quality* of classroom communication may account for up to 25 percent of achievement variance. Added to the 65 percent contributed by student ability and motivation, it is possible to account for 90 percent of the variance in student achievement. These linkages are summarized in figure 4-1, a model of learning in the classroom.

A feature of the argument just developed needs to be underscored. The limits on the contribution of the quality of classroom communication to student achievement have been specified in terms of the contribution of a teacher interacting with students during an academic term. Thus, the theory minimizes the true impact of classroom communication on learning. Student ability and student motivation in grade 7, for example, is at least partially a function of the quality of classroom communication during grades K-6.

Assuming the validity of this theory of classroom learning, a logical question which arises is: Why has research had such a difficult time identifying features of classroom communication which predict student achievement? Gage (1978) argues persuasively that this situation is an artifact of research which maximizes Type II Error (failure to reject a false null hypothesis). His reasoning: First, as our theory of classroom learning posits, classroom communication accounts for up to 25 percent of achievement variance. It is unreasonable, therefore, to expect any single variable to account for a substantial portion of the variance in student achievement. Since a correlation of .5 is needed to account for 25 percent of the variance, the correlation of any single variable with achievement will, for the most part, range from + .1 to + .4. Second, most studies of classroom interaction are, of necessity, studies of relatively small numbers of teachers. Gage, for example, cites Dunkin and Biddle's 1974 summary of nineteen studies of the relationship between teacher indirectness and student achievement where the number of teachers ranged from eight to seventy, with a median of fifteen. Only five of the nineteen studies used samples consisting of more than eighteen teachers. Third, an examination of Cohen (1977) indicates that for a sample consisting of fifteen teachers, the correlation coefficient must equal .51 to be significant at the .05 level; .64 to be significant at the .01 level. Gage's conclusion: "It seems evident that most of the single studies should not be expected to yield statistically significant results. Thus, with such sample sizes, we shall almost never reject the null hypothesis (the hypothesis that the true correlation is zero) even when it is false" (p. 27).

TEACHING AS PROBLEM SOLVING

Assuming, then, that classroom communication affects learning in ways that we can—but have not yet—discovered, we derive a fourth reaction—teaching as problem solving. Such a position has implications for both teachers and researchers.

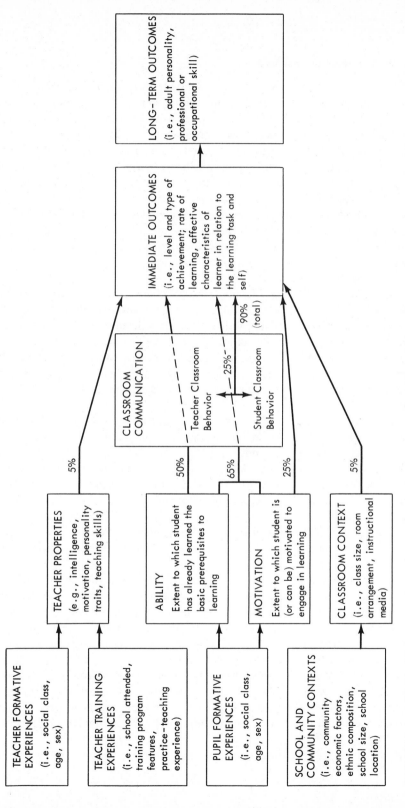

FIGURE 4-1 A Model of Classroom Learning (Adapted from Dunkin and Biddle, 1974, p. 38.)

Implications for Teachers

Since teachers must continue to operate in advance of a data base, they must become researchers who develop creative and innovative approaches to teaching which they try and test in their classrooms. The role of the teacher, then, becomes that of researcher and problem solver. In exercising this role, teachers need to be aware of the most recent theory and research on instruction as a means of enlarging the number and quality of options available for testing. It is important, for example, that teachers are aware that nine variables have yielded consistent results across the fifty-odd studies in which naturally occurring teacher behavior was related to measures of student growth (Rosenshine & Furst 1973): (1) clarity, (2) variability, (3) enthusiasm, (4) task-oriented and/or businesslike attitude, (5) criticism, (6) teacher indirectness, (7) student opportunity to learn criterion material, (8) use of structuring comments, and (9) multiple levels of questions or cognitive discourse.

The temptation to consider these variables obvious, if not trite, is offset by the realization that a number of other seemingly plausible and virtuous sounding variables have *not* correlated well with student achievement: nonverbal approval, praise, warmth, the I/D ratio, or ratio of all indirect teacher behaviors (acceptance of feelings and ideas, praise, and questions) to all direct teacher behaviors (lecture, directions, and criticism), questions or interchanges classified into only two cognitive types, student talk, and student participation (Rosenshine & Furst 1973).

It must be acknowledged that the results cited above are largely correlational in nature. Thus, we do not know, for example, whether (1) students learn more when teachers are indirect, (2) teachers are more indirect when students demonstrate more learning, or (3) additional, unspecified variables produce both indirectness and achievement. While the research necessary to untangle such overlapping relationships is progressing, Rosenshine (1970) was able to locate only fifteen studies in which teachers were trained to teach a class of students in a specific manner, observational measures were collected to verify that teachers behaved as intended, and end of experiment measures (such as achievement scores) were obtained.

Rosenshine and Furst's nine variables, then, are nine dimensions of classroom communication which teachers can try and test in their classrooms. As they engage in this process of inquiry, teachers should be aware of the role that student participation can play as an index of their success. Bloom (1976, p. 123) cites data that when the class group is the unit for assessing participation, the correlation with either final achievement or gain in achievement is very similar: .27; when the individual's participation is observed or measured, the correlation with final achievement is .42, while the correlation with gain in achievement is .58. Since, therefore, about 20 percent of the variation in achievement of individuals is accounted for by their participation in the classroom learning process, participation is a convenient way for the teacher to assess the quality of classroom communication. While it is likely that this participation must be overt for young children to learn, covert participation—if it is ensured—is highly effective for older learners.

Implications for Researchers

For researchers, teaching as problem solving implies a strong commitment to conceptualizing and executing the sophisticated, systematic research programs needed to generate an adequate data base. Three important components of such an effort are synthesizing existing research, increasing the quantity of research, and improving the quality of research.

Synthesizing existing research.   The case for synthesizing existing research has been made earlier in this essay. Because most studies of classroom interaction are, of necessity, studies of small numbers of teachers and because expected correlations and differences are small, it is often not possible to reject a false null hypothesis. Thus, if we are to make sense of classroom interaction research, it is necessary to move the focus of attention from the results of a single study to a focus on the patterns which emerge from all of the studies in a particular area of research. Gage (1978) and his colleagues, for example, recently sifted through the detailed information for several hundred variables in four major correlational studies of teaching. As a result of their meta-analysis, they were able to specify, among others, the following set of inferences as to how third grade teachers should work if they wish to maximize achievement in reading for children either high or low in academic orientations. As a next step, then, they included these variables in an experimental treatment designed for the third grade level.

1. Teachers should have a system of rules that allow pupils to attend to their personal and procedural needs *without* having to check with the teacher.
2. Teachers should move around the room a lot, monitoring pupils' seatwork *and* communicating to their pupils an awareness of their behavior, while also attending to academic needs.
3. When pupils work independently, teachers should insure that the assignments are interesting and worthwhile yet still easy enough to be completed by each third grader working without teacher direction.
4. Teachers should keep to a minimum such activities as giving directions and organizing the class for instruction. Teachers can do this by writing the daily schedule on the board, insuring that pupils know where to go, what to do, etc.
5. In selecting pupils to respond to questions, teachers should call on a child by name *before* asking the question as a means of insuring that all pupils are given an equal number of opportunities to answer questions.
6. With *less* academically oriented pupils, teachers should always aim at getting the child to give some kind of response to a question. Rephrasing,

giving cues, or asking a new question can be useful techniques for bringing forth some answer from a previously silent pupil or one who says "I don't know" or answers incorrectly.

7. During reading-group instruction, teachers should give a maximal amount of brief feedback and provide fast-paced activities of the "drill" type. (p. 39)

Anderson and others (1979), following a similar procedure, identified and tested the following guidelines for teaching first grade reading groups:

1. Once in (reading) group, the children should be seated with their backs to the rest of the class while the teacher is facing the class.
2. The introduction to the lesson should contain an overview of what is to come to mentally prepare the students for the presentation.
3. The teacher should work with one individual at a time in having the child practice the new skill and apply the new concept, making sure that everyone is checked and receives feedback.
4. The teacher should use a pattern for selecting children to take their turns reading in the group or answering questions (such as going from one end of the group to the other) rather than calling on them randomly and unpredictably.
5. When call-outs occur, the teacher should remind the child that everyone gets a turn and that he or she must wait his or her turn to answer.
6. After asking a question, the teacher should wait for the child to respond and also see that other children wait and do not call out answers. If the child does not respond within a reasonable time, the teacher should indicate that some response is expected by probing.
7. Praise should be used in moderation. The teacher should praise thinking and effort more than just getting the answer, and should make praise as specific and individual as possible.
8. Criticism should also be as specific as possible, and should include specification of desirable or correct alternatives.

These attempts at synthesis share two features: (1) they integrate existing correlational findings from large scale studies and (2) the integrated findings are then assessed in experimental studies where treatment conditions are tested for success in producing more learning than in control groups and for generalization to contexts beyond basic skills instruction in the elementary grades. As the Gage and Anderson lists demonstrate, this approach produces nonintuitive results, and researchers therefore need to continue this effort at synthesizing and testing existing research. One aid in this process is Glass's (1977) description of a sophisticated methodology for integrating findings through the meta-analysis of research.

Increasing the quantity of research. Far too much of the research which exists is fragmented, one-study research. Rosenshine (1976), for example, was able to identify only eleven groups of researchers engaged in programmatic studies of the relationship between classroom instruction and student achievement within the process-product paradigm.

1. David Berliner, Charlie Fisher, and Len Cahen—Far West Laboratory; Walter Borg—Utah State University
2. Jere Brophy and Carolyn Evertson—Texas Research and Development Center in Teacher Education
3. Homer Coker—Carrolton State College, Georgia, and Don Medley—University of Virginia
4. N. L. Gage—Stanford Research and Development Center in Teaching
5. Meredith Gall, William Tikunoff, and Betty Ward—Far West Laboratory
6. Tom Good—University of Missouri
7. Gene Hall, Sue Loucks, Gary Borich, and Robert Peck—Texas Research and Development Center in Teaching
8. Gaea Leinhardt, Margaret Wang, and William Cooley—Learning Research and Development Center, University of Pittsburg
9. Fred McDonald—Educational Testing Service
10. Robert Soar—University of Florida
11. Jane Stallings—Stanford Research Institute

That this situation is not unique to classroom interaction research is demonstrated by a recent report of Marshall Arlin (1977) who conducted an authorship study of the seven hundred plus journals referenced in the Current Index to Journals in Education (CIJE), a service of the Educational Resources Information Center (ERIC) based on a computer tape containing all entries from January, 1969 to January, 1977. Allocating one FPE (full-publication equivalent) to each article (thus, dual authorship = .50 FPE for each author), the 100,400 authors distributed themselves as follows:

TABLE 4-1

NUMBER OF PUBLICATIONS	PERCENTILE FOR FPE	PERCENTILE FOR NUMBER OF AUTHORS
.5	29%	
1.0	78%	75%
1.5	82%	
2.0	90%	88%
2.5	92%	
3.0	95%	93%
4.0	97%	96%
5.0	98%	97%
6-7	99%	98%
8-52*	99+%	99%

*highest FPE = 49

As can be seen from table 4-1, 75 percent of all authors publishing articles in the past eight years have been one-study authors. This 75 percent is comprised of 46 percent sole authors and 29 percent coauthors. If a criterion of four articles (96 percent) or three FPE's (95 percent) is used as a lower limit indicator of cumulative research, then only 4 to 5 percent (or 10 percent allowing for error) of those publishing in the past eight years would qualify as engaging in cumulative inquiry. The mean FPE is 1.31 (SD = 1.52) and the mean total publications is 1.61 (SD = 1.76).

Compounding the severity of this situation is the fact that largely because of federal government funding policies, most of the programmatic research has focused on studies of the early elementary grades. As a result, we know less about the impact of classroom interaction at the secondary school level and almost nothing about it at the college or university level. What is needed, then, is a commitment to programmatic research at all educational levels.

Improving the quality of research. A number of recent essays have provided many practical suggestions for improving the quality of classroom interaction research. Two individuals who synthesize many of the better suggestions are Berliner (1976), who provides a good summary of the impediments to the study of teacher effectiveness for the dominant approach to classroom interaction research (the process-product paradigm) in terms of instrumentation problems, methodological problems, and statistical problems; and Doyle (1977), who suggests two alternative paradigms—a mediating process paradigm derived mainly from prose-learning research and a classroom ecology paradigm constructed from naturalistic studies of school life. Additional suggestions for conceptualizing and executing sophisticated, systematic research programs are provided by Dunkin and Biddle (1974), Nuthall (1974), Borich (1977), Furlong and Edwards (1977), Winne and Marx (1977), Berliner (1978), Cooley (1978), Gage (1978), and Munby and Wilson (1978).

SUMMARY

This chapter has focused on research concerning classroom interaction—teachers and students talking together for purposes of learning—conducted within the process-product paradigm. After seventy years of such research, students of the classroom have become increasingly precise in their description of what occurs there. It is now possible, for example, to describe the "moves" of classroom interaction (structuring, soliciting, responding, reacting) and the principles which guide their application. We know, for example, that the teacher does approximately two-thirds of the talking—much of which involves asking questions and commenting on student responses. The majority of these questions require little thought on the part of students (about 60 percent of teacher's questions require students to recall facts, about 20 percent require students to think, and the remaining 20 percent are procedural). While students are asked to respond no more than six or seven times an hour, they are expected to pay attention to the progress of the lesson. When students do respond to teacher questions, their response is either repeated, praised, or otherwise commented on by the teacher. In short, most of the student's time in the typical classroom is taken up in listening to other students' responses and the teacher's comments on those responses.

Despite this ability to predict what *will happen* in the classroom, it is only within the past few years that it has been possible to hope for the discovery of principles or guidelines which can be used to specify what *should happen* there. Contributing to this new hope are a number of large scale correlational studies which have produced findings which researchers have integrated into treatment packages that were then tested for (1) success in producing more learning than what is observed in control groups and (2) for generalization to contexts beyond basic skills instruction in the elementary grades. To facilitate the speedy development of guidelines which will improve instruction, it will be necessary for researchers to commit themselves to conceptualizing and executing research programs which are sophisticated and programmatic. Three components of such an effort are (1) synthesizing existing research, (2) increasing the quantity of research, and (3) improving the quality of research. In the meantime, because teachers must teach in the absence of useful guidelines for effective teaching, it is important that they be trained to become researchers who develop creative and innovative approaches to teaching which they try and test in their classrooms.

SUGGESTED READINGS

BROPHY, J. E., and T. L. GOOD. *Teacher-Student Relationships: Causes and Consequences.* New York: Holt, Rinehart and Winston, 1974.

A summary of the authors research program focused on the kinds of individual differences in students that make differential impressions upon teachers, the ways that such differential impressions lead teachers to form differential attitudes and expectations regarding different students, and the ways that these differential teacher attitudes and expectations begin to affect teacher-student interaction patterns.

DUNKIN, M. J., and B. J. BIDDLE. *The Study of Teaching.* New York: Holt, Rinehart & Winston, 1974.

A summary of the methods, concepts, and findings of observational research on teaching.

FLANDERS, N. A. *Analyzing Teaching Behavior.* Reading, Mass.: Addison-Wesley Publishing Co., Inc., 1970.

A summary of the methods, concepts, and findings of research using Flanders's system of Interaction Analysis.

GAGE, N. L. *The Scientific Basis of the Art of Teaching.* New York: Teachers College Press, 1978.

A collection and extension of three Julius and Rose Sachs Memorial Lectures given at Teachers College in April of 1977 which explore the status and future of the field of research on teaching.

MEDLEY, D. M. *Teacher Competence and Teacher Effectiveness: A Review of Process-Product Research.* Washington, D.C.: American Association of Colleges for Teacher Education, 1977.

An analysis and synthesis of the results of research studies on teacher competence and teacher effectiveness.

PETERSON, P. L., and H. H. WALBERG (eds.) *Research on Teaching: Concepts, Findings, and Implications.* Berkeley, Calif.: McCutchan, 1979.

A collection of essays addressed to researchers which concern the history of empirical research on teaching, its present status, and possible directions for the future.

SIMON, A., and E. G. BOYER (eds.) *Mirrors for Behavior III: An Anthology of Observation Instruments.* Wyncote, Pa.: Communication Materials Center, 1974.

An anthology of ninety-nine systems used in observational research on teaching.

REFERENCES

ADAMS, R. S. "Observational studies of teacher role." *International Review of Education,* 1972, *18,* 440–58.

ANDERSON, L., and others. "An experimental study of effective teaching in first grade reading groups." *Elementary School Journal,* 1979, *79,* 193–223.

ARLIN, M. "One-study publishing typifies education inquiry." *Educational Researcher,* 1977, *6,* 11–15.

BARR, A. S., and others. "The validity of certain instruments employed in the measurement of teaching ability." In H. M. Walker (ed.), *The Measurement of Teaching Efficiency.* New York: Macmillan, Inc., 1935, pp. 73–141.

BELLACK, A. A., and others. *The Language of the Classroom.* New York: Teachers College, Columbia University, 1966.

BERLINER, D. C. "Clinical studies of classroom teaching and research." Paper presented at the annual meeting of the American Educational Research Association, Toronto, 1978.

BERLINER, D. C. "Impediments to the study of teacher effectiveness." *Journal of Teacher Education,* 1976, *27,* 5–13.

BERLINER, D. C., and N. L. GAGE. "The psychology of teaching methods." In N. L. Gage (ed.), *The Psychology of Teaching Methods.* Chicago: University of Chicago Press, 1976.

BLOOM, B. S. *Human Characteristics and School Learning.* New York: McGraw-Hill Book Company, 1976.

BORICH, G. D. "Sources of invalidity in measuring classroom behavior." *Instructional Science,* 1977, *6,* 283–318.

CLIFFORD, G. .J. "A history of the impact of research on teaching." In R. M. W. Travers (ed.), *Second Handbook of Research on Teaching.* Chicago: Rand McNally & Company, 1973.

COHEN, J. *Statistical Power Analysis for the Behavioral Sciences* (2nd ed.). New York: Academic Press, Inc., 1977.

COLEMAN, J. S., and others. *Equality of Educational Opportunity.* Washington, D. C.: Government Printing Office, 1966.

COOLEY, W. W. "Explanatory observational studies." Paper presented at the annual meeting of the American Educational Research Association, Toronto, 1978.

DAHLLOF, U. S., and V. P. LUNDGREN. "Project Compass 23: Macro and micro approaches combined for curriculum process analysis: A Swedish educational field project." Paper presented at the annual meeting of the American Educational Research Association, Minneapolis, 1970.

DOYLE, W. "Paradigms for research on teacher effectiveness." In L. S. Shulman (ed.), *Review of Research in Education,* Vol. 5. Itasca, Ill.: F. E. Peacock, 1977, pp. 163–98.

DUBIN, R. and T. C. TREVEGGIA. *The Teaching-Learning Paradox: A Comparative Analysis of College Teaching Methods.* University of Oregon: Center for Advanced Study of Educational Administration, 1968.

DUNKIN, M. J., and B. J. BIDDLE. *The Study of Teaching.* New York: Holt, Rinehart & Winston, 1974.

FURLONG, V. A., and A. D. EDWARDS. "Language in classroom interaction: Theory and data." *Educational Research,* 1977, *19,* 122–28.

GAGE, N. L. "Theories of teaching." In E. R. Hilgard (ed.), *Theories of Learning and Instruction,* N.S.S.E. Yearbook No. 63, Part 1. Chicago: University of Chicago Press, 1964.

GAGE, N. L. *The Scientific Basis of the Art of Teaching.* New York: Teachers College Press, 1978.

GALL, M. D. "The use of questions in teaching." *Review of Educational Research,* 1970, *40,* 707–21.

GALLAGHER, J. J. "Three studies of the classroom." In J. J. Gallagher and others (eds.), *Classroom Observation,* American Educational Research Association Monograph Series on Curriculum Evaluation, Monograph No. 6 Chicago: Rand McNally & Company, 1970.

GLASS, G. V. "Integrating Findings; the Meta-Analysis of Research." In L. S. Shulman (ed.), *Review of Research in Education,* V. 5. Itaska, Ill.: F. E. Peacock, 1977. 351–79.

GOOD, T. "Teacher effectiveness in the elementary school: What we know about it now." *Journal of Teacher Education,* 1979, *30,* 52–64.

HEATH, R. W., and M. A. NIELSON. "The research basis for performance-based teacher education." *Review of Educational Research,* 1974, *44,* 463–84.

HIGHET, G. *The Art of Teaching.* New York: Vintage Books, 1954.

HOETKER, A. J., and W. P. AHLBRAND. "The persistence of recitation." *American Educational Research Journal,* 1969, *6,* 145–69.

JACKSON, P. W. *Life in Classrooms.* New York: Holt, Rinehart & Winston, 1968.

JENCKS, C., and others. *Inequality: A Reassessment of Family and Schooling in America.* New York: Basic Books, 1972.

KRATZ, H. E. "Characteristics of the best teachers as recognized by children." *Pedagogical Seminary,* 1896, *3,* 413–18.

MEDLEY, D. M. "Early history of research on teacher behavior." *International Review of Education,* 1972, *18,* 430–39.

MOSTELLER, F., and D. P. MOYNIHAN. *On Equality of Educational Opportunity.* New York: Vintage Books, 1972.

MUNBY, H., and R. WILSON. "Convergent and discriminant validity of classroom observation instruments: Conceptual background, critique, and a case in point." *The Alberta Journal of Education Research,* 1978, *24,* 69–80.

NUTHALL, G. "Is classroom interaction research worth the effort involved?" *New Zealand Journal of Educational Studies,* 1974, *9,* 1–17.

NUTHALL, G., and I. SNOOK. "Contemporary models of teaching." In R. M. W. Travers (ed.), *Second Handbook of Research on Teaching.* Chicago: Rand McNally & Company, 1973.

ROSENSHINE, B. "Experimental classroom studies of teacher training, teacher behavior, and student achievement." Paper presented at the annual meeting of the National Council for the Social Studies, New York, 1970.

ROSENSHINE, B. "Recent research on teaching behavior and student achievement." *Journal of Teacher Education,* 1976, *27,* 61–64.

ROSENSHINE, B., and N. FURST. "The use of direct observation to study teaching." In R. M. W. Travers (ed.), *Second Handbook of Research on Teaching.* Chicago: Rand McNally & Company, 1973.

STEVENS, R. *The Question as a Measure of Efficiency in Instruction.* Contributions to Education No. 48. New York: Teachers College, Columbia University, 1912.

WALLEN, N. E., and R. M. W. TRAVERS. "Analysis and investigation of teaching methods." In N. L. Gage (ed.), *Handbook of Research on Teaching.* Chicago: Rand McNally & Company, 1963.

WINNE, P. H., and R. W. MARX. "Reconceptualizing research on teaching." *Journal of Educational Psychology,* 1977, *69,* 668–78.

CHAPTER FIVE
CLASSROOM ENVIRONMENTS AND NONVERBAL BEHAVIOR

William R. Todd-Mancillas*

*Dr. Todd-Mancillas is Assistant Professor, Department of Human Communication, at Rutgers University.

INTRODUCTION

There are perhaps nearly seventy extant textbooks on educational psychology (Biehler 1971). Nearly all of these texts concern themselves with providing an overview of contemporary and classic learning theories and attendant research activities, with some of them purporting to provide practical advice for classroom teachers. However, this author is unable to find even one such textbook giving serious attention to environmental factors affecting learning processes.

The lack of attention given to physical learning environments is further illustrated by the fact that despite the occasional attention given to open classroom design, the vast majority of American classrooms are much as they were seventy years ago—square or rectangular rooms containing under- or oversized desks arranged in rows and columns, with the walls painted uninspiring moss green or insipid grey, and with few furnishings or artistic artifacts unrelated to formal teacher-student interactions.

A serious problem arises from lack of sufficient attention given to the physical aspects of classroom learning environments. First, lack of attention given to the physical environment is tacit endorsement for the status quo emphasis on developing learning theories, curriculum design, testing, and evaluation procedures. Of course these latter concerns are important, but no less so than the context, including physical context, in which the results of these research activities are implemented. During the last fifteen years, the Department of Architecture, University of Michigan, has compiled several compendiums of abstracts describing scores of ways in which environmental modifications significantly impact upon learning processes and outcomes (Educational Facilities Laboratories, Inc. 1965; Pastalan 1974; King & Marans 1979), and we would do well to translate these findings into workable recommendations for modifying classroom environments.

The purpose of this chapter is to call attention to some of the environmental factors most likely to affect learning outcomes. Specific recommendations are made, relevant to seven dimensions of physical learning environments: space, time, sound, temperature, color, lighting, and artifacts. These dimensions are discussed because they are relatively easy to modify and because there is increasing empirical support for their importance in affecting learning processes and outcomes.

SPACE

Excess Classroom Space

Because of declining enrollments throughout the country, many schools are finding themselves in the position of having excess space. While the preferred alternative for using this excess space might be to reduce class sizes, budget limitations make this an unrealistic possibility for most school districts and universities. Accordingly, alternative usage for these spaces must be found and preferably ones that would result in means of defraying cost of running the schools. One alternative is to make available to the public some of these classroom, auditorium, and gymnasium spaces on a rental basis. For instance, in Eugene, Oregon, the Lincoln Elementary School was scheduled for demolition for failure to meet current building code regulations. Instead, the city offered to pay for the costs of upgrading the school, provided that space be allotted for a community development office, an outreach clinic, a senior citizen's center, and a day-care center (Brooks 1979).

Implementing alternative uses of school learning spaces has several other advantages. One is that students are made more aware of the outside world. Their proximity to activities atypical of traditional learning environments, but highly typical of community activities, makes it possible for them to develop fuller and more realistic understandings of the world in which they live. Also, allowing outside agents to participate in the school programs makes it possible for a school to upgrade its image. Since citizens have greater opportunity to see what is going on in the schools, they will also have greater opportunity to verify their understanding of school operations and probably have a more vested interest in the school's continuance and development.

Seating Arrangements

In general, one should arrange seating in accordance with the degree of teacher-student and student-student interactions appropriate for the realization of specified learning objectives. Traditional row and column arrangements (see figure 5-1*a*) are appropriate in those instances where listening and note taking are the preferred instructional activities (Sommer 1977). Modular arrangements

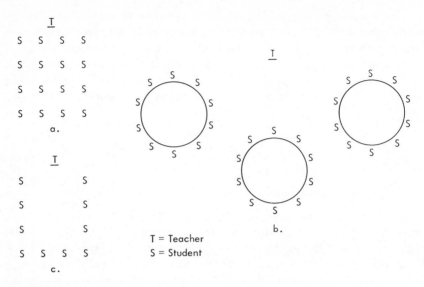

FIGURE 5-1

(see figure 5-1*b*) are appropriate for facilitating multiple small group inter-actions, such as when students are divided in several small groups and all are working independently toward resolution of a given problem (Hurt, Scott, & McCroskey 1978). For purposes of encouraging discussion among the greatest number of students, a circular or horseshoe arrangement (see figure 5-1*c*) is preferred (Mehrabian & Diamond 1971; Patterson and others 1979).

These suggestions follow from a proposition now well established in the small group interaction literature: the more visual information one has about other group participants, the more likely one is to engage in verbal interaction with the other participants (Heston & Garner 1972; Batchelor & Goethals 1972; Hendrick, Giesen, & Coy 1974; Giesen & McClaren 1976). Moreover, there may be a slightly greater tendency for women than men to desire or need more direct seating orientations as a condition for facilitating maximum interaction (Ellsworth & Ross 1975; Patterson 1978).

Involving Students in
Classroom Design

In designing and implementing not only spatial modifications, but any environmental modification, teachers and administrators are advised to solicit input from students and parents. Soliciting and incorporating student and pa-rental input increases the probability of identifying appropriate modifications (Sommer 1977), and of obtaining endorsement from students, the persons most affected by the innovation (Rogers & Shoemaker 1971; Havelock and others 1973).

Barbato (1979) explains how student involvement can be accomplished effectively even at the fourth grade level. At the Church Street Elementary School in White Plains, New York, a program has been implemented whereby professional architects teach elementary school students theories and skills of architectural design. After an introduction to basic concepts of usage of space, color, decor, and temperature as they affect human behavior, students identify a given architectural problem and systematically evaluate and implement appropriate solutions. One such problem concerned the construction of an in-class activity center. Students were divided into six teams of three members each, and each designed an activity space appropriate for meeting previously specified objectives. Students then evaluated each of the six proposals, decided upon the preferred alternative, and subsequently implemented this alternative.

One of the most important benefits of involving students in environmental decision making is that they assume responsibility for modifying an environmental factor of vested interest to themselves. Owing to the personal relevance of the learning experience, the students are more likely to retain and implement this information in the future, when related problems emerge calling for the evaluation of an environmental problem and the design and implementation of appropriate solutions (Biehler 1971). This approach is also in keeping with the need for education to encourage students to not only learn technical skills, but also to be able to identify important problems and design and implement solutions appropriate for their constructive resolution (Bruner 1966). If students as young as ten and eleven years old are able to modify successfully their learning environment, then there is no reason to believe that older students are any less competent.

TIME

Teaching Schedules

Teaching schedules should be varied as much as possible. This is a particularly relevant concern for elementary school teachers. While high school and college students have some freedom of choice about subject selection and time of day when they can take particular courses, elementary school children have virtually no freedom of choice. Hurt, Scott, and McCroskey (1978) advise that inflexible teaching schedules are particularly harmful to "owl" children, children that are less alert during morning hours and who become more alert as the day progresses; other children are less adversely affected by inflexible schedules, but they too would probably benefit from the variety induced by occasionally varying sequence of lesson plans. In any event, unless some diversity in teaching schedules is introduced, owl children will not have equal opportunity to grasp subjects covered only during the early morning hours.

Whenever possible, recesses should be scheduled *before* lunch periods.

Sellers (1978) reports that this modification greatly reduces the amount of roughhousing behavior typical in many elementary school cafeterias. The prior lunch break gives children an opportunity to work off constructively the tension resulting from several consecutive hours of frequently tedious activity in sitting positions.

Time Consultants and Teaching Schedules

Appropriate personnel should consider hiring outside consultants to analyze time expenditures in the school system. At least one case study establishes that this is probably worthwhile. Using trained classroom observers, the Austin (Texas) school district conducted a survey of time expenditures in twenty Title I schools (Davidson & Holley 1979). Analysis of 1,457 observation hours indicated that nearly half of the 6-hour school days were occupied by such noninstructional activities as "listening to announcements; taking out and putting away supplies; bathroom trips; discipline; or simply waiting for teacher instruction." This was an alarming finding in light of the fact that related research demonstrates a positive correlation between learning and the amount of time allotted to and engaged in instruction (Fisher, Marliave, & Filby 1979).

After a series of instructional modifications resulting from ongoing consultation with the University of Texas Research and Development Center for Teacher Education, the Austin School District was able to increase daily instructional time by twenty-three to thirty-four minutes, the equivalent of lengthening a school year by ten to sixteen days. Davidson and Holley (1979) estimate this increased instructional time resulted in minimal savings to tax payers of about $2,142,000. Perhaps more importantly, there were also achievement gains in reading and mathematics.

Pausing for Student Responses

Teachers should allow at least ten to fifteen seconds for students to respond to teachers' questions before answering the questions themselves. Some students need more time to think about a question before responding, and it is frustrating for them to mentally construct a response, with the intention of publicly responding, only to have that opportunity snatched away from them by an impatient teacher (Hurt, Scott, & McCroskey 1978).

SOUND

Music and Student Cooperation

Playing soothing music is one means of generating positive affect and cooperative behavior. Fried and Berkowitz (1979) conducted a study comparing willingness to engage in helpful behaviors as a function of being exposed to aversive music condition or a control condition where no music was played. Fried and Berkowitz interpret these results as support of previous findings suggesting a positive correlation between soothing music and heightened pleasant interactions (Barmel 1973; Chertock 1974; Preueter & Mezzano 1973).

While this study was conducted using college students, it is reasonable to assume soothing music would have similar effects on younger students. The present author recalls vividly a related experience while working as a teacher's aide for the Whittier Elementary School in Long Beach, California. One teacher at this school used music as both a reinforcer to reward preferred student behaviors and also as a means of diffusing tension. Instead of setting aside one or two hours weekly to study music, this teacher rewarded attentive behavior by playing the harpsichord for about ten minutes, once or twice daily. Naumann (1977) also notes the facilitative impact music may have in establishing suitable class moods and counteracting classroom boredom.

While it is not possible for all teachers to play musical instruments, it is possible for most teachers to play cassette recordings of students' favorite music selections, perhaps even recordings of music created by students themselves.

Noise and Younger Students

It is important that relatively quiet learning environments be availed younger students (kindergarten age and younger) having excessively noisy home environments. Heft's (1979) research strongly suggests that for young children, noisy home environments are correlated significantly with inferior attention and learning abilities. Specifically, he compared kindergarten age children living in home environments (Altoona, Pennsylvania) with children living in less noisy home environments (Bellewood, Pennsylvania), and found that Bellewood children performed significantly better than Altoona children on concentration and visual search tasks. Similar results have been obtained for nursery school children (Turnure 1970).

While teachers and administrators have little or no control over home environments, they have considerable control over learning environments. Accordingly, it seems reasonable to suggest their giving special consideration in providing more quiet and pleasant sound environments for younger children having excessively noisy home environments. Moreover, this recommendation is probably of more relevance for students living in urban than residential or rural neighborhoods. As a rule of thumb, educators should provide learning environments with noise levels not in excess of 100 decibels, as allied research suggests impaired learning performance occurs at and above this level (Kassinove 1972).

Noise and Older Students

For older children, beyond first or second grade, educators need not devote excessive attention and money toward reducing noise levels below a moderately noisy level (70 to 90 decibels). This recommendation is based on the results of several studies in which results fail to establish negative relationships between moderate noise levels and older students' performances on arithmetic problems (Park & Payne 1963; Kassinove 1972), reading performance (Slater 1968), and performance on a clerical numbers test (Super, Braasch, & Shay 1947).

TEMPERATURE

Temperature and Learning

Classroom temperature should be maintained between 66°F and 72°F to assure optimal performance when students are engaged in mental and physical activities. Predominate support for this recommendation derives from Harner's (1973) comprehensive review of research assessing the impact of thermal variations on learning among elementary and secondary school students. In addition to his comprehensive review of the literature, Harner's own research suggests that students between the ages of eight and eleven experience significant decreases in reading speed and comprehension when classroom temperature rises above 77°F. Harner's conclusion is that maximally effective learning is most likely to take place in classroom environments with temperatures ranging between 68°F and 74°F. The first recommended range differs slightly from Harner's because an attempt is being made to modify Harner's suggested range in accordance with more current thinking about optimal temperature ranges for learning environments. For instance, Rosenfeld (1977) cites a recommendation by Kowinski (1975) suggesting that a more effective range lies between 64°F and 68°F.

Of course, one cannot speak intelligently of optimal temperature control without also taking into consideration wide variations in humidity. When there are seasonal variations in humidity, optimal temperature will vary as well. Partridge and MacLean (1935) conducted a study wherein twenty-five Canadian school children (ages seven and fourteen) performed a variety of mental and physical tasks, including drawing and game playing, under varying temperature and humidity conditions. Results indicated that during the summer months, with humidity levels approximating 50%, students felt most comfortable when classroom temperatures approximated 70°F. However, during the winter months, with humidity levels approximating 35%, students felt most comfortable when classroom temperatures approximated 66°F.

Humidity and Absenteeism

During winter months, classroom humidity should not fall below 30% or above 50%, as humidity levels either above or below this range are associated with student illness and absenteeism. Green (1979) reviewed seven studies assessing the impact of humidity variations on frequency of illness and absenteeism among children and adult populations. Five of these studies demonstrated increased illness and absenteeism associated with decreased humidity in the classroom or work environment. Green's own study was the most comprehensive of those reviewed. He studied 3,600 children (grades 1 to 8) attending 11 different schools in Saskatoon, Canada. Results indicated that children attending schools with classroom humidities ranging between 22% and 26% experienced nearly 13% greater illness and absenteeism than children attending schools with classrooms having humidity levels ranging between 27% and 33%. While these findings are suggestive of preferences for increased humidity in the classroom, Green also cautions against excessive humidity, as allied research also indicates that increased respiratory infections result from humidity levels in excess of 50%.

Air Conditioning and Learning

As a means of regulating temperature in classroom environments, serious effort should be made to provide air conditioning in the classroom, especially during the summer months. Nolan (1960) compared military students' performance levels during the winter months, in classrooms heated to optimal temperature levels, with performance levels during summer months, when students experienced physical discomfort because of excessively high temperatures. Findings indicated students earned significantly higher grades during the winter than summer months, presumably because greater temperature control was available during the winter.

McDonald (1960) investigated teacher and student attitudes and performance levels as a function of having or not having air conditioning. Results indicated that air conditioning had a significant effect on reducing teacher and student fatigue, and reduced fatigue, in turn, was associated with increased student attention and effective use of study time.

COLOR

Optimal Classroom Color Schemes

For younger students (elementary school age) classrooms should be painted warm colors, including yellow, peach, and pink, while for older students (secondary school age and older) classrooms should be painted cooler colors, including blue and blue-green (Thompson 1973). Rosenfeld (1977) summarizes research done by Ketcham (1958) establishing empirical support for the proposition that learning is affected by variations in color of classroom environments. Three different schools were painted different colors to assess the impact of color schemes on kindergarten children's behavior and learning. One school was not painted even though it needed painting. A second school was painted with light buff walls and white ceilings. A third school was, as Rosenfeld describes

... painted in accordance with principles of color dynamics—corridors were painted a cheerful yellow with grey doors and mop boards; classrooms with northern exposure were painted a pale rose, while those facing south were painted in cooler shades of blue and green; front walls were painted darker than side walls; the art room was painted a "neutral" grey so as to avoid interfering with the colorful work which it contained; and green chalkboards were installed to reduce glare.

In each of these schools student behavior was systematically observed and recorded during the following two years. Results indicated that students in the third school experienced significant improvement in social habits, health and safety habits, language arts, arithmetic, social studies, science, and music. Students attending the unpainted school demonstrated the least improvement, suggesting that even simple changes in color schemes can positively affect learning.

Rosenfeld and Civikly (1976) discuss a second study done by the Connecticut Department of Education (1966) assessing learning, behavior, and attitudes over a period of several years, and determined that students feel more pride when attending schools with refurbished color schemes. This increased pride, in turn, appeared to be associated with decreased vandalism and other behavioral problems.

Burgoon and Saine (1978) cite research discussed by Silden (1973) suggesting that IQ scores can be dramatically affected by variations in classroom color. One group of children played in warm, bright colored rooms; a second group of children played in rooms painted white, black, or brown. Children playing in warm colored rooms experienced a 12 point increase in IQ while children playing in the white, black, or brown rooms experienced a 14 point drop in IQ scores.

Color and Learning Materials

When it is not possible to repaint classrooms, teachers should make a special effort to incorporate color variations in the actual learning and testing materials. Lombard and Riedel (1978) found that students with learning difficulties (ages eight to sixteen) obtained significant increases in Wechsler Intelligence scores when the tests were printed using blue and red ink on a white background rather than the traditional black ink on a white background.

Involving Students in Color Design

Whenever possible, students should be directly involved in the planning and implementation of color changes in their learning environments (Swanson & Curtis 1973). Displeased with the "eye-case green" walls in their high school classroom, Aminah Clark, a psychology teacher, solicited the assistance of Joan Swanson, an art teacher, for the purpose of decorating one of the walls with a mural. Students designed and painted a mural in the classroom which, the teachers report, did much to increase student morale and demonstrate to the students they could apply in a meaningful way what they had read and studied about the history and psychology of art. Further, having applied abstract concepts by physically manipulating the environment, students increased the probability of retaining the information they learned. Everett (1973) reports a similarly successful effort involving middle school students in the decorating of school walls.

LIGHTING

Full- versus Reduced-Spectrum Lighting

Whenever possible, avoid usage of ordinary reduced-spectrum fluorescent lighting and use instead either incandescent or full-spectrum fluorescent lighting (Dusky 1978). Dusky describes a study done in Sarasota, Florida, which compared the effects of limited versus full-spectrum fluorescent lighting on the behavior and learning abilities of first graders. Two classes used conventional, reduced-spectrum fluorescents; two classes used full-spectrum fluorescents. In the conventional lighting condition, the children experienced significantly greater nervous fatigue, irritability, lapses of attention, hyperactivity, and decreased classroom performance than in the full-spectrum condition. Interestingly, the first graders in the full-spectrum condition also developed significantly fewer dental cavities.

Relevant to the discussion of preferences for full-spectrum over reduced-spectrum lighting is the question of preference for artificial versus natural light sources. While many educators have expressed the opinion that natural light sources are preferable to artificial light sources and, moreover, that artificial light sources are in fact associated with a wide range of maladies and learning disorders, available evidence is inconclusive, and caution should be exercised in recommending one source in preference to the other.

Larson (1966) supervised a three-year study assessing the impact of windowless versus fenestrated classrooms on student learning and behavior. Two schools (kindergarten through third grade) were used in the study. The findings indicated nonsignificant differences between the fenestrated and windowless classroom conditions with respect to measures of reading, spelling, writing, arithmetic, and artwork. While most of the children expressed indifference as to preferences for windowless versus fenestrated classrooms, teachers overwhelmingly preferred windowless classrooms, primarily because windowless classrooms allowed for increased storage, shelving, and display surfaces. Teachers also preferred windowless classrooms because they did not provide students with the opportunity to be distracted by passers-by or inclement weather.

One negative difference did emerge, however, warranting further study and evaluation. Kindergarten children were absent significantly more frequently in the windowless school condition than were either the first, second, or third graders also attending the windowless school, or children of all ages attending the fenestrated school. Larson and his colleagues are unable to provide a fully satisfactory explanation for the differences in frequency of absences, but suggest that it may have been attributed to parents being reluctant to send their younger children to an experimental school.

Involving Students in Lighting Design

Students should be allowed maximum opportunity to modify their lighting environments (Hayward 1974). Hayward explains that most person-made environments use static lighting systems—that is, systems disallowing modification of light intensity or hues. These static systems prevent users (students and teachers) from making constructive lighting adjustments in response to psychological, social, task, or climatic variables. The amount of light generated by the typical classroom lighting system is the same regardless of whether it is a sunny or cloudy day, whether students are engaged in activities requiring cooperative effort or individual activity, or whether one is sitting in an area of the classroom (usually a corner) requiring more light than other areas.

Static lighting systems are at variance with one of the most fundamental propositions for effective physical environments: Individuals seek maximum control over their physical environments and when prevented from exercising this control, there is frequently a diminishing in quality of their work and interpersonal relationships (Proshansky, Ittelson, & Rivlin 1970). Fiske and Maddi (1961) take a similar position when they discuss self-regulated stimulus modifications as constituting an important class of "varied experiences," crucial to healthy psychological growth and productive adaptation to social and physical environments.

The Importance of Contrast

In choosing hues and intensity of lighting schemes, care should be exercised in selecting appropriate contrasting schemes. Frequently, "contrast (the comparison of object reflectance with background reflectance) so greatly affects visual acuity and visual performance (speed and accuracy) that . . . contrast . . . is more important than level of illumination" (Guth 1962; Hayward 1974). In fact, one of the most common problems in designing suitable lighting environments is not insufficient wattage, but the "underuse of different light sources and inflexibility and lack of variety in lighting arrangements" (Zarkas and Miner, 1977). Zarkas and Miner further advise that marked contrasts between lit and unlit areas are especially fatiguing and recommend dimmers to control for optimal contrast effects. Note that if several dimmers were available in the same classroom, one dimmer for each of the several lights, then students would be availed some opportunity to construct optimal contrast conditions. Moreover, allowing students to choose their own seating locations increases the probability that they will have the amount and type of lighting most suited to their needs.

Educators might do well to consider lighting and contrasting schemes employed by socially responsive business and industry, as these schemes may suggest novel approaches for lighting designs in educational settings. For instance, Vincent Sardi (1979) provides interesting insight into how his famous restaurant is designed to impart a mood suitable for enjoyable eating and conversation.

> The decor is a restaurant's way of telling its patrons where they are. And we want ours to be completely devoid of harshness. For this reason we have no neon or fluorescent lights, which I think are simply horrible for the faces of women and especially elderly men. We have parchment shades around every light bulb, we bounce most of the light off the ceiling, and we raise and lower its intensity during the restaurant's hours so it doesn't look dingy at lunch hour, or overly bright in the evening. In short, the decor at Sardi's is adjusted to minimize jarring harshness and the main purpose is to communicate a sense of comfort.

This statement reflects a few of the key recommendations already made in this chapter. Through the use of table lamps, users are provided with some measure of control over their lighting environments. Further control is availed through the use of dimmers to regulate overall light sources in accordance with times of day and purpose of social interactions. But most importantly, those in a position of power, the restaurant owners and managers, are keenly aware of client needs and are making serious efforts to modify the restaurant environment in accordance with those needs. Educators would do justice to their mission were they to adopt a similar perspective and also experiment with constructive modifications in the physical environment, not only with respect to lighting and contrast, but with respect to all other environmental factors as well.

ARTIFACTS

Beautiful versus Ugly Classrooms

To facilitate positive classroom interactions, educators should select and arrange in aesthetically pleasing fashion furnishings and other artifacts lending a pleasing ambiance to the learning environment.

Maslow and Mintz (1956) conducted one of the classic studies demonstrating the potential impact of room aesthetics on human behavior. Students were asked to rate photographic negatives of several faces in one of three rooms. The beautiful room was 11' X 14' X 10' and had two large windows, beige walls, carpet, drapes, indirect lighting, and attractive furnishings. The ugly room was small, 7' X 12' X 10', and had two half windows, battleship-grey walls, an overhead bulb with a dirty torn, ill-fitting shade, and disheveled furnishings. The third room, a control condition, was similar to offices provided for many college and university professors. It was 15' X 17' X 10', with three windows, grey walls, indirect lighting, and ordinary office furniture, neither particularly attractive nor ugly.

Analysis of the data indicated that students in the beautiful room rated the stimulus faces as having significantly greater energy and well being than did students working in either the ugly or average room. Moreover, ratings obtained in the average room were only slightly higher than ratings obtained in the ugly room, a finding compatible with a basic tenet underlying contemporary human communication theory: The absence of decidedly positive feedback is perceived as the presence of negative or nonreinforcing feedback (Wilmot 1975). On the basis of these and related findings obtained from similar investigations (Wong & Brown 1923; Mintz 1956; Bilodeau & Scholsberg 1959), we conclude that it is not sufficient to merely remove from the learning environment markedly ugly artifacts. In addition, educators must introduce into the learning environment artifacts perceived as aesthetically pleasing by students and teachers alike.

Perhaps more important than the particular artifacts found in a learning environment is the degree of neatness with which they are arrayed (Campbell 1978). Campbell had students rate slide presentations of sixteen office conditions, the conditions varying from one another in terms of (a) presence or absence of plants and fish, (b) presence or absence of art objects, (c) degree of neatness in the environment, and (d) furniture arrangement.

The results indicated students felt most comfortable, at ease, and welcomed in the office that was neat, and slightly less so in the offices with living things and art objects. The arrangement of furniture was significantly less effective in eliciting heightened ratings than any of the other variables. While these results were obtained for student evaluations of faculty offices, they are nonetheless suggestive of student responses to neat versus cluttered classroom environments, and emphasize the importance of maintaining classroom furniture and equipment in good repair.

Student Constructed Artifacts

Since there is considerable variability in student preferences and lifestyles (Feldman & Newcomb 1976), it is extremely difficult for any one teacher to predict for any one class the artifacts most likely to complement student needs and learning objectives. There are several ways in which students can assist in this decision-making process. They can be involved in the selection of classroom furniture and equipment at the time purchasing decisions are made, or they can be involved in the actual construction of classroom furnishings. Taylor and Swentzel (1979) describe how an entire high school was constructed using in large part student and teacher labor and ingenuity, including the design and construction of school benches, desks, and other school furnishings.

Another way in which students can assist in the beautification of classroom environments is through the display of art objects that they create themselves. Examples include student constructed calligraphic images which not only beautify walls but also help students to learn spelling (Cataldo 1979), student designed picture stories to complement their creative writing (Olson & Wilson 1979), student constructed fabric patchworks that also relate to history lessons about self-reliance and community comradery during the founding years of our republic (Hersey 1977), and usage of formal display centers allowing art students to experience firsthand the difficulties and rewards experienced by professional artists in their attempts to gain public recognition and support (Zeven & Bauman 1977).

It is the contention of many art educators (for example, Reid 1976) that most students graduate from high school and college without fully appreciating that analogic (artistic) expression is equally as relevant as digital (linguistic and linear) expression of culture and the human condition. Students would be more likely to appreciate the relevance of artistic expression if they were more directly involved in developing artistically expressive skills, particularly when the results of these efforts are used to beautify their own personal learning and living environments.

Wolfgang (1977) explains the special relevance of displaying student art to minority students. All too frequently, students from ethnic minorities are made to feel that their culture is of substantially lesser importance than the dominant culture. This feeling of self-disparagement results not so much from the presence of definitive messages actively besmirching minority cultures as it does from the absence of assertive mechanisms portraying and giving positive weight to their culture.

By displaying student art, students of all ethnic and cultural backgrounds are provided an opportunity to constructively modify and identify positively with their learning environments. In addition, associated discussions may illustrate to all students how artistic objects reflect the essences of the associated culture, a point vividly illustrated in Zastrow's (1979) discussion of Papago baskets and Acoma clay pots. The Papago and Acoma American Indians are famous for their simply, yet beautifully, designed pots and baskets. Their construction is illustrative of three essential features of Papago and Acoma culture: successful reliance upon natural resources for survival; an ability and need to intertwine beauty with functional activities, and the considerable patience needed to design and construct their baskets and pots.

SUMMARY

This chapter examined environmental factors impacting upon learning processes. The chapter began with a discussion of the need to attend equally as much to the physical environments in which learning takes place as the teacher-student interactions transpiring within those environments. Specific suggestions were made for modifying classroom space, time, sound, temperature, color, lighting, and artifacts—all of which have been demonstrated to affect significantly student behaviors within learning settings. Some of the key observations follow:

Classroom Space: Excess space can be put to good advantage by soliciting usage by community offices not usually affiliated with public schools. This might prove an effective way of increasing school revenues while at the same time improving images of public schools.

Classroom Time: Student behaviors can frequently be modified in desirable ways by simply reordering the sequence of instructional and noninstructional activities. Time consultants can be used to identify potentially constructive modifications.

Classroom Sound: Traditional teaching orientations would have us believe that classroom noise is to be avoided. However, available research suggests that noise may only be a serious problem for some types of students, particularly young students, and that certain sounds (for example, soothing music) may even be conducive to learning.

Classroom Temperature: Optimal classroom temperatures lie between 66°F and 72°F, with humidity also playing a key role in affecting student attentiveness and absenteeism. Air conditioning is noted as a particularly important means of maintaining high teacher and student morale.

Classroom Color: Classroom color can easily affect learning and interaction moods and as with all environmental variables, optimal usage of color varies as a function of context and student preferences. In general, younger students will probably benefit more from warm colors, including yellow, peach, and pink, while older students might benefit more from cooler colors, including blue and blue-green.

Classroom Lighting: Whenever possible, every effort should be made to use full- versus reduced-spectrum lighting, as reduced-spectrum lighting has been found to be associated with eye strain and anxiety. One also need note that lighting contrast is equally as important as the type and intensity of light used.

Classroom Artifacts: Much can be done to beautify and increase the comfort of classrooms through judicious selection of furniture and art objects. Also, as with all environmental variables, owing to individual difference in needs and aesthetic preferences, it is appropriate to involve students to the fullest extent possible in selecting and maintaining classroom artifacts.

SUGGESTED READINGS

DEPARTMENT OF ARCHITECTURE, UNIVERSITY OF MICHIGAN. *SER 1 Environmental abstracts.* New York: Educational Facilities Laboratories, Inc., 1965.

This is a highly readable and well-organized source book of studies on the impact of environmental factors on learning. Over six hundred studies are abstracted and evaluated. The writing is clear, and particular studies are easily located by using the author and subject indexing systems.

DUSKY, LORRAINE. "Startling new theories on light and color." *Popular Mechanics,* September 1968, *150* (3), 180–86.

This is a highly readable and current synthesis of studies done assessing light and color variables on human development and behavior, and is particularly useful as a cursory introduction for undergraduate students.

GALLOWAY, C. M. Special issue on nonverbal communication in the classroom. *Theory into Practice,* June 1977, *16* (3), entire issue.

This entire issue of *TIP* consists of sixteen articles by prominent experts on nonverbal communication, and each author discusses the implications of his or her research to improving classroom learning. Included among the contributors are Charles M. Galloway, Edward T. Hall, Robert Rosenthal, Lawrence Rosenfeld, Russell L. French, and Martha Davis.

GREEN, G. H. "Ah-choo! Humidity can help." *American School and University,* September 1979, *52* (1), 64–65.

Though brief and without adequate documentation, this is the most current and complete article describing the need for moderate amounts of humidity in classrooms, especially during the winter months.

HAYWARD, G. "Psychological factors in the use of light and lighting in buildings." In J. Lang, C. Burnette, W. Moleski, & D. Vachon (eds.), *Designing for Human Behavior: Architecture and the Behavioral Sciences.* Stroudsburg, Pa.: Dowden, Hutchinson, and Ross, Inc., 1974.

This is an excellent discussion of lighting principles and the limits placed on our knowledge in consequence of inadequate research. The bibliography is complete and accurate.

HURT, H. THOMAS, D. MICHAEL SCOTT, and JAMES C. McCROSKEY. *Communication in the Classroom.* Reading, Mass.: Addison-Wesley Publishing Co., Inc., 1978.

This is a highly readable and pragmatic overview of verbal and nonverbal communication processes affecting learning. Students typically report this book as a valuable resource aid and preferred over the more expensive, bulky, and less current educational textbooks addressing some of the same issues.

KING, J., and R. W. MARANS. *The Physical Environment and the Learning Process.* Ann Arbor, Mich.: Architectural Research Laboratory and Institute for Social Research, 1979.

This is not the most complete—but it is the most current—compilation of abstracts describing studies assessing the impact of environmental variables on learning processes.

LARSON, C. T. *The Effect of Windowless Classrooms on Elementary School-children.* Ann Arbor, Mich.: Architectural Research Laboratory, University of Michigan, 1966.

This publication describes a three-year study assessing the effects of windowless classrooms on learning and classroom behavior among elementary school children. This study stands as a model for excellence in field research, and would be appropriate reading for graduate courses in nonverbal communication.

MASLOW, A. H., and N. L. MINTZ. "Effects of esthetic surroundings: Initial effects of three esthetic conditions upon perceiving 'energy' and 'well-being' in faces." *Journal of Psychology*, 1956, *41*, 247–54.

This is perhaps the best known for the "ugly" versus "beautiful" room studies, and should be required reading for students in nonverbal communication courses, both at the undergraduate and graduate levels.

PASTALAN, L. A. (ed.) *Man-Environment Reference Environmental Abstracts.* New York: Educational Facilities Laboratory, 1974.

This is another comprehensive collection of abstracts describing and evaluating studies assessing the impact of environmental factors on learning. It has a neat format, and the indexing system facilitates easy identification of pertinent studies.

REFERENCES

BARBATO, J. "A Secret of Inner Space," *American Education.* July, 1979 V. 15 (6) p. 23–27.

BARMEL, L. N. "Psychiatrist as music therapist." *Journal of Music Therapy*, 1973, *10*, 93–85.

BATCHELOR, J. P., and G. R. GOETHALS. "Spatial arrangements in freely formed groups." *Sociometry*, 1972, *35*, 270–79.

BIEHLER, R. F. *Psychology Applied to Teaching.* Boston: Houghton Mifflin Company, 1971.

BILODEAU, J. M., and H. SCHLOSBERG. "Similarity in stimulating conditions as a variable in retroactive inhibition." *Journal of Experimental Psychology*, 1959, *41*, 199–204.

BROOKS, A. "Sharing: A solution to excess space?" *Teacher*, February 1979, *96*, 59–60.

BRUNER, J. S. *Toward a Theory of Instruction.* New York: W. W. Norton & Co., Inc., 1966.

BURGOON, J. K. *The Unspoken Dialogue: An Introduction to Nonverbal Communication.* Boston: Houghton Mifflin Company, 1978.

CAMPBELL, D. E. "Interior office design and visitor response." Paper presented at the annual meeting of the American Psychological Association, Toronto, Canada, August-September, 1978.

CATALDO, J. W. "Structuring ideas through calligraphic images." *School Arts,* September 1979, *79,* 10–15.

CHERTOCK, S. L. "Effect of music on cooperative problem-solving by children." *Perceptual and Motor Skills,* 1974, *39,* 986.

CONNECTICUT DEPARTMENT OF EDUCATION, "School building finishing and economy," The School Building Economy Series, No. 6. Hartford, Conn.: State Department of Education, June, 1966.

DAVIDSON, J. L., and F. M. HOLLEY. "Your students might be spending only half of the school day receiving instruction." *The American School Board Journal,* March 1979, *166,* 40–41.

DEPARTMENT OF ARCHITECTURE, UNIVERSITY OF MICHIGAN, *SER I Environmental abstracts.* New York: Educational Facilities Laboratories, Inc. 1965.

DUSKY, L. "Startling new theories on light and color." *Popular Mechanics,* September 1968, *150,* 180–86.

ELLSWORTH, P. C., and L. ROSS. "Intimacy in response to direct gaze." *Journal of Experimental Social Psychology,* 1975, *11,* 592–613.

EVERETT, T. "May we have the walls." *School Arts,* November 1973, *73,* 26–27.

FELDMAN, K. A., and T. M. NEWCOMB. *The Impact of College on Students.* San Francisco: Jossey-Bass Inc., Publishers, 1976.

FISHER, C., R. MARLIAVE, and N. N. FILBY. "Improving teaching by increasing 'academic learning time.'" *Educational Leadership,* 1979, *37* (1), 52–54.

FISKE, D. W., and S. R. MADDI. *Functions of Varied Experience.* Homewood, Ill.: Dorsey Press, 1961.

FRIED, R., and L. BERKOWITZ. "Music hath charms . . . and can influence helpfulness." *Journal of Applied Social Psychology,* 1979, *9,* 199–208.

GIESEN, M., and H. A. McCLAREN. "Discussion, distance, and sex: Changes in impressions and attraction during small group interactions." *Sociometry,* 1976, *39,* 60–70.

GREEN, G. H. "Ah-choo! Humidity can help." *American School and University,* September 1979, *52,* 64–65.

GUTH, S. K. "Lighting research." *American Industrial Hygiene Association Journal,* 1962, *23,* 359–71.

HARNER, D. P. "A review of research concerning the thermal environment and its effects on learning." Dissertation, University of Mississippi, 1973.

HAVELOCK, R. G., A. GUSKIN, M. FROHMAN, M. HAVELOCK, M. HILL, and J. HUBER. *Planning for Innovation through Dissemination and Utilization of Knowledge.* Ann Arbor, Mich.: Center for Research on Utilization of Scientific Knowledge, 1973.

HAYWARD, G. "Psychological factors in the use of light and lighting in buildings." In J. Lang, C. Burnette, W. Moleski, and D. Vachon (eds.), *Designing for Human Behavior: Architecture and the Behavioral Sciences.* Stroudsburg, Pa.: Dowden, Hutchinson, and Ross, Inc., 1974.

HEFT, H. "Background and focal environmental conditions of the home and attention in young children." *Journal of Applied Social Psychology,* 1979, *9,* 47–69.

HENDRICK, C., M. GIESEN, and S. COY. "The social ecology of free seating arrangements in a small group interaction context." *Sociometry,* 1974, *37,* 262–274.

HERSEY, E. M. "Patchwork patterns." *Teacher,* January 1977, *94,* 64–65.

HESTON, J. K., and P. GARNER. "A study of personal spacing and desk arrangement in a learning environment." Paper presented at the annual meeting of the International Communication Association, Atlanta, Georgia, 1972.

HURT, H. THOMAS, MICHAEL D. SCOTT, and JAMES C. McCROSKEY. *Communication in the Classroom.* Reading, Mass.: Addison-Wesley Publishing Co., Inc., 1978.

KASSINOVE, H. "Effects of meaningful auditory stimulation on children's scholastic performance." *Journal of Educational Psychology,* 1972, *63,* 526–30.

KETCHAM, H. *Color Planning for Business and Industry.* New York: Harper and Row, 1958.

KING, J., and R. W. MARANS. *The Physical Environment and the Learning Process.* Ann Arbor, Mich.: Architectural Research Laboratory and Institute for Social Research, 1979.

KOWINSKI, W. "Shedding new light," *New Times,* March 7, 1975, *4,* 46.

LARSON, C. T. *The Effect of Windowless Classrooms on Elementary School Children.* Ann Arbor, Mich.: Architectural Research Laboratory, University of Michigan, 1966.

LOMBARD, T., and T. RIEDEL. "Analysis of factor structure of the WISC-R and the effect of color on the coding subtest." *Psychology in the Schools,* 1978, *15,* 176–79.

McDONALD, E. G. "Effect of school environment on teacher and student performance." *Air Conditioning, Heating, and Ventilation,* 1960, *57,* 78–79.

MASLOW, A. H., and N. L. MINTZ. "Effects of esthetic surroundings: Initial effects of three esthetic conditions upon perceiving 'energy' and 'well-being' in faces." *Journal of Psychology,* 1956, *41,* 247–54.

MEHRABIAN, A., and S. G. DIAMOND. "Effects of furniture arrangement, props, and personality on social interaction." *Journal of Personality and Social Psychology,* 1971, *20,* 18–30.

MINTZ, N. L. "Effects of esthetic surrounds: Prolonged and repeated experience in a 'beautiful' and 'ugly' room." *Journal of Psychology,* 1956, *41,* 459–66.

NAUMANN, N. "Three cheers for the self-contained classroom." *Teacher,* September 1977, *95,* 86–89.

NOLAN, J. A. "Influence of classroom temperature on academic learning." *Automated Teaching Bulletin,* 1960, *1.*

OLSON, J. L., and B. WILSON. "A visual narrative program—grades 1–8." *School Arts,* September 1979, *79,* 26–33.

PARK, J. F., and M. C. PAYNE. "Effects of noise level and difficulty of task in performing division." *Journal of Applied Psychology,* 1963, *47,* 367–68.

PARTRIDGE, R. C., and D. L. MacLEAN. "Determination of the comfort zone for school children." *Journal of Industrial Hygiene,* 1935, *17,* 66–71.

PASTALAN, L. A. (ed.) *Man-Environment Reference Environmental Abstracts.* New York: Educational Facilities Laboratory, 1974.

PATTERSON, M. L. "The role of space in social interaction." In A. Siegman and S. Feldstein (eds.), *Nonverbal Behavior and Communication.* Hillsdale, N.J.: Lawrence Erlbaum Associates, 1978.

PATTERSON, M. L., C. E. KELLY, B. A. KONDRACKI, and L. J. WULF. "Effects of seating on small group behavior." *Social Psychology Quarterly,* 1979, *42,* 180–85.

PREUETER, B. A., and J. MEZZANO. "Effects of background music on initial counselor interaction." *Journal of Music Therapy*, 1973, *10*, 205–12.

PROSHANSKY, H. M., W. H. ITTELSON, and L. G. RIVLIN. "Freedom of choice and behavior in a physical setting." In P. Ittelson and L. Rivlin (eds.), *Environmental Psychology: Man and His Physical Setting*. New York: Holt, Rinehart & Winston, 1970.

REID, L. A. "Feeling and aesthetic knowing." *Journal of Aesthetic Education*, 1976, *10*, 11–28.

ROGERS, E. M., and F. F. SHOEMAKER. *Communication of Innovations*. New York: Free Press, 1971.

ROSENFELD, L. B. "Setting the stage for learning." *Theory into Practice*, 1977, *16*, 167–73.

ROSENFELD, L. and J. CIVIKLY. *With Words Unspoken*. New York: Holt, Rinehart & Winston, 1976.

SARDI, V. "Sardi's: Something beyond food." In R. W. Budd and B. Ruben (eds.), *Beyond Media*. Rochelle Park, N.J.: Hayden Book Company, 1979.

SELLERS, J. "How to improve lunchtime discipline." *The American School Board Journal*, July 1968, *165*, 29.

SILDEN, I. "Psychological effects of office planning." *Mainliner*, December 1973, 30–34.

SLATER, B. R. "Effects of noise on pupil performance." *Journal of Educational Psychology*, 1968, *59*, 239–43.

SOMMER, ROBERT. "Classroom layout." *Theory into Practice*, June 1977, *16*, 174–75.

SUPER, D. E., W. F. BRAASCH, and J. B. SHAY. "The effect of distractions on test results." *Journal of Educational Psychology*, 1947, *38*, 373–77.

SWANSON, J., and D. CURTIS. "Just the thought of painting a wall excites me." *School Arts*, November 1973, *73*, 12–13.

TAYLOR, A., and R. SWENTZEL. "The Albuquerque Indian school: Culture, environment and change." *School Arts*, October 1979, *79*, 12–16.

THOMPSON, J. J. *Nonverbal Communication in the Classroom*. New York: Citation Press, 1973.

TURNURE, J. "Children's reactions to distractors in a learning situation." *Developmental Psychology*, 1970, *2*, 115–22.

WILMOT, W. W. *Dyadic Communication: A Transactional Perspective*. Reading: Mass.: Addison-Wesley Publishing Co., Inc., 1975.

WOLFGANG, A. "The silent language in the multicultural classroom." *Theory into Practice*, 1977, *16*, 145–52.

WONG, H., and W. BROWN. "Effects of surroundings upon mental work as measured by Yerkes' multiple choice method." *Journal of Comparative Psychology*, 1923, *3*, 319–31.

ZARKAS, P., and M. MINER. *Lifespace*. New York: Macmillan, Inc., 1977.

ZASTROW, L. M. "Native American art forms and value systems." *School Arts*, October 1979, *79*, 41.

ZEVEN, J., and R. K. BAUMAN. "Art in a community college." *School Review*, 1977, *86*, 96–103.

CHAPTER SIX
NONVERBAL IMMEDIACY IN INSTRUCTION

Peter Andersen and Janis Andersen*

*Dr. Peter Andersen is a visiting lecturer and Dr. Janis Andersen is Associate Professor, Department of Speech Communication, at San Diego State University.

INTRODUCTION

The learning process is complex and difficult to characterize in its entirety. In fact, educators have generally agreed that the outcomes produced by the learning process are not singular in focus. In 1948, at a meeting of the American Psychological Association in Boston, a group of scholars interested in college testing and evaluation began labeling and defining learning dimensions. Their goal was to create a widely shared theoretical framework for communicating about various kinds of learning. Their efforts resulted in a three-part taxonomy of learning which is widely accepted today. Learning has a cognitive domain, an affective domain, and a psychomotor domain (Bloom and others 1956).

The Learning Domains

These scholars never claimed that a threefold dimension of learning typologies was a new idea. In fact, they report that such a division is as ancient as Greek philosophy, with philosophers and psychologists repeatedly describing similar divisions: cognition, conation, and feeling; thinking, willing, and acting; and so on (Krathwohl, Bloom, & Masia 1964). What the 1948 committee created was not a new idea but rather a precise language to facilitate communication about an old idea—the dimensions of learning.

The cognitive domain of learning deals with the attainment of knowledge and the acquisition of intellectual and analytical abilities and skills. This domain is concerned with a person's ability to recall, comprehend, apply, analyze, synthesize, and evaluate cognitive information. This domain is the most obvious concern of educators, or at least it has been the focus of most evaluation activity.

The affective domain is concerned with student likes and dislikes, attitudes, values, beliefs, appreciations, and interests. It is concerned with teaching effects which have some "emotional overtone" (Kibler, Barker, & Miles 1970). Although most educators would subscribe to the importance of the affective domain, little attention has been focused on specific methods for improving affective outcomes.

The third domain is the psychomotor domain. This domain emphasizes muscular or motor skill and is mainly concerned with a student's ability to reproduce a neuromuscular coordination task. This domain is highly important for some learning tasks and less relevant for others.

Teacher Behavior and
the Learning Domains

In any learning environment, it is difficult to isolate learning goals into one of the three domains. Oftentimes these domains overlap, and most educators simply accept the fact that cognitive, affective, and psychomotor skills are often interrelated and are mutually and reciprocally affected by a learning activity. Most of the time, however, educators focus attention on one of the domains and measure achievement or learning outcomes for that domain alone. When only one domain is assessed, attention is usually focused on the cognitive domain. Since we view this situation as unfortunate, this chapter will focus primarily on the affective domain of instruction and will suggest ways to promote better affective outcomes.

The affective domain is centered around the creation of positive feelings. Krathwohl, Bloom, and Masia (1964) wrote a book which laid the foundation for the classification of the affective domain. In that book they note that there had been an implicit assumption that if cognitive objectives were met, there would be a corresponding meeting of affective goals. They cite evidence and arguments to show that this assumption simply is not true. In fact, sometimes cognitive information occurs at the expense of affective behaviors. For example, a college student may learn to recognize the work of classical composers in a music appreciation class but may develop an aversion to classical music as a result. Just as the development of cognitive behaviors is dependent on tasks specifically designed for cognitive goals, affective behaviors develop in the same way. They result from learning experiences appropriately designed to instill or provide for affective outcomes.

One important way to promote positive affective outcomes is to create a communication context which produces positive feelings between teachers and students. The verbal and nonverbal communication messages that teachers employ have an important effect on students' liking for the teacher, the subject matter, and the discipline area. For example, Andersen (1979) found that half of the variation in student liking for teachers was associated with the kind of nonverbal communication the teachers employed. Specifically, teachers who employ nonverbal immediacy behaviors concurrently communicate positive affect.

DEFINING NONVERBAL IMMEDIACY

Nonverbal immediacy or intimacy behaviors are nonlinguistic actions which send four simultaneous and complementary messages.

1. *Immediacy behaviors are approach behaviors.* Mehrabian (1971a) maintains that immediacy in behavior comes across in a number of abbreviated forms of approach as opposed to avoidance. For example, a wave of the hand is an abbreviated grasp or handshake, and a pat on the back is an abbreviated hug.

2. *Immediacy behaviors signal availability for communication.* Goffman (1964) suggests that these behaviors generally come in sets which signal social accessibility. For example, moving close to someone, facing them, and establishing eye contact are immediacy behaviors and signal to another person that communication is about to take place.

3. *Immediacy behaviors increase sensory stimulation.* Patterson (1978a) reports that physiological and psychological arousal result from immediacy behaviors such as reduced distance, touching, or eye contact. Mehrabian (1971a) suggests that immediacy behaviors involve an increase in overall sensory stimulation and are typically multichanneled.

4. *Immediacy behaviors communicate interpersonal closeness and warmth.* A number of researchers (Andersen 1979; Exline & Winters 1965; Mehrabian 1971a) have noted that immediacy behaviors produce interpersonal closeness and reduce psychological distance in positive relationships.

NONVERBAL IMMEDIACY BEHAVIORS

Now that the general definition of immediacy has been discussed, our attention will focus on specific nonverbal behaviors that communicate immediacy.

Proxemics

Proxemics is the use of interpersonal space and distance. Whenever anyone communicates, their distance and angle from the receiver communicate powerful messages, including varying degrees of warmth or immediacy. At least two proxemic cues are thought to signal immediacy during communication: (a) physical distance, and (b) the angle or orientation of the communicators.

Physical distance in the classroom. Mehrabian and Friar (1969) found that communicators stand closer to people they like than to those they dislike. Similarly, Mehrabian and Ksionzky (1970) report that in a series of studies, closer distances result in more positive attitudes. Indeed, Michael Argyle (1972) suggests that intimacy is primarily a function of five nonverbal cues, the first being physical proximity. Many teachers fail to establish much immediacy or interpersonal closeness with a class because they remain physically remote. Standing at the front of the room or sitting behind a desk is common behavior for teachers. In these remote positions, it is quite difficult for a teacher to develop a close relationship with a class, even if the teacher wants to develop such a relationship. Indeed, Schusler (1971) reports an unpublished study which maintains that nervous, insecure elementary teachers establish their territory around their desk, whereas confident teachers use the entire room and frequently move among their students.

Body angle in the classroom.   The second proxemic behavior that signals immediacy is body angle or body orientation. More immediacy is communicated when two or more interactants face one another (Andersen, Andersen, & Jensen 1979; Mehrabian 1971a). Less immediacy is conveyed in side-by-side positions, and the back-to-back position is least immediate. Indeed, when individuals feel too intimate or immediate, they will reduce the directness of body orientation. A whole group of studies indicate that when one person gets too close proxemically, the other person will compensate with a less direct body orientation (Harper, Wiens, & Matarazzo 1978; Patterson 1973, 1977). Many teachers do not fully face their class when teaching. They hide behind desks, podiums, and tables, and often continuously write on the blackboard, with their backs to the class. Not only does this reduce the immediacy between teachers and their classes, it also removes any visual communication between the teacher and the class. In this situation, the teacher cannot see behavior problems, fails to receive any nonverbal communication from the class, and cannot field questions or comments. Experienced teachers learn to do most of their blackboard work before class and spend the largest amount of their teaching time facing their classes.

Other proxemic behaviors.   While considerable research has demonstrated that both distance and body orientation are important components of proxemic immediacy, other such behaviors may be discovered in the future. One such behavior which may be a component of immediacy is whether two communicators interact on the same physical plane. Tall elementary teachers tower above their students. Many teachers have indicated that sitting or squatting while interacting with their students increases the immediacy of the interaction. Roger Brown (1965) has suggested that interacting on the same plane is a manifestation of interpersonal solidarity, a similar construct referencing closeness. While this idea seems intuitively pleasing, research is needed in the elementary school to determine if immediacy is increased by interacting on the same level or physical plane.

Haptics

Haptics or tactile communication involves the use of physical contact between people. Previous research has included tactile messages as an important part of immediacy or interpersonal closeness (Andersen 1979; Andersen,

Andersen, & Jensen 1979; Mehrabian 1971a; Patterson 1977). In a study of married couples, Beier and Sternberg (1977) reported that couples who experienced the least disagreement touched themselves less and touched each other more frequently than couples who frequently disagreed. Several recent books on instructional communication suggest that touch can have a very positive impact, particularly in the elementary classroom (Bassett & Smythe 1979; Hurt, Scott, & McCroskey 1978; Thompson, 1973).

Types of classroom touch.   What types of touch should and should not be used in the classroom? This depends on the age of the students involved. In the early elementary school years, teachers act as surrogate parents, and large quantities of touch are permitted and probably expected. Since touch is one of the most immediate, intimate forms of communication (Montague 1970; Morris 1971; Thompson 1973), tactile contact may be necessary for the elementary teacher to convey love and affection to students. Indeed, Hurt, Scott, and McCroskey (1978) suggest that when a teacher withholds touch, a child may feel isolated and rejected. On the other hand, intimate, loving touches are not expected or condoned by the school or community at the junior high school or high school level, since they are often equated with sexual behaviors.

A number of tactile behaviors can be used at any level from elementary school through college. Since touch is a very personal form of communication, handshakes and shoulder touches can convey immediacy, while rarely being interpreted as a sexual come-on. Similarly, pats on the back and other nonthreatening forms of touch can serve as powerful reinforcers in a way that talk or high grades simply cannot. Finally, instrumental or functional touches occur frequently in school, particularly in classes where psychomotor skills are being taught, including shop courses, athletics, dance, art, and even when learning such skills as handwriting. While the primary purpose of instrumental touch is purely task related, this form of tactile communication probably conveys immediacy as well.

Constraints on the use of touch.   Teachers who employ touch should be aware of the school and community norms governing such behavior. Furthermore, since many people in American culture are highly touch-avoidant (Andersen & Leibowitz 1978), teachers should be aware that touch is not reinforcing or pleasurable to some students. Moreover, teachers who are themselves touch avoiders must find other ways of communicating immediacy and may wish to avoid teaching early elementary grades, where touch is common if not inevitable.

Vocalics

Vocalic or paralinguistic communication deals with the nonverbal elements of the human voice. When people talk they communicate verbally, or linguistically, through words, and nonverbally, or nonlinguistically, through the way in which the words are spoken. Additionally, various nonverbal vocal utterances (for example, uh-huh, mmm, eeek) have meaning even though these utterances are not accompanied by any verbal communication.

Vocal behaviors and immediacy.   Vocalic communication is an important determiner of immediacy. Generally, communicators who vary the pitch, loudness, and tempo of their speech are viewed as more immediate. In an imaginative study, Scherer (1979) used a Moog synthesizer to electronically vary pitch, amplitude, duration, and speed (tempo) of nonverbal sounds. The results showed that the best emotional and affective cues were the result of changes in pitch and tempo. In a series of studies (Mehrabian 1971a; Mehrabian & Ferris 1967), it was discovered that interpersonal liking is in large part a function of vocal cues and facial cues rather than verbal cues. In factor-analytic studies of nonverbal behavior, Andersen, Andersen, and Jensen (1979) found vocal expressiveness to be an important part of communicated immediacy. Voices which are expressive, enthusiastic, and varied (particularly in pitch and tempo) seem to convey the most immediacy.

Classroom effects of laughing.   Another vocal behavior which probably communicates interpersonal immediacy is laughing. Considerable literature exists indicating that laughing operates physiologically as a tension reducer and contributes to relaxation, especially during tense interactions. Trager (1958) recognized laughing as one of a class of nonverbal, parlinguistic cues called vocal characterizers, but little research has followed this initial attempt. An early study by Barr (1929) which examined the qualities of good and poor social science teachers found that "good" teachers laughed more, including laughing along with the class. While future research is necessary, it seems that teachers who are more willing to laugh communicate more immediacy.

Kinesics

Kinesics is communication that occurs via body movement and most likely is the richest source of immediacy cues. Kinesics includes all body movements that have meaning for receivers, including overall body tension, walking, leaning, head position and movements, facial expressions, and hand gestures.

Teacher smiling.   One of the most powerful immediacy cues is the smile. Researchers have consistently classified smiling as central to the concept of immediacy (Andersen, Andersen, & Jensen 1979; Mehrabian 1971a; Patterson 1978a), intimacy (Argyle 1972), or warmth (Reece & Whitman 1962). Smiling has been found to produce substantial positive therapeutic effects in relationships, including an increase in interpersonal acceptance (Reece & Whitman 1962). Mehrabian (1971b) demonstrated that positive facial affect, including smiling, was one of the primary ways by which affiliativeness was communicated. Indeed, when Rosenfeld (1966a, 1966b) had subjects simulate how they would communicate affiliativeness, smiling was one of the most commonly used behaviors. When one person smiles, the other frequently smiles in return (Kendon 1967; Rosenfeld 1966a, 1967), indicating that smiles are reciprocal immediacy behaviors. Gutsell and Andersen (1980) reported data which showed that as sources increased the amount of smiling, they were perceived as more immediate and affiliative. Moreover, more subjects returned post cards indicating that they would attend a party when the hostess smiled a greater percentage of the time. Positive facial expressions were found to communicate affiliation in a series of studies (Mehrabian 1970, 1971a; Mehrabian & Ferris 1967). Teachers who frequently smile are communicating immediacy in one of the easiest and most powerful ways. Students in all grade levels are sensitive to smiles as a sign of positive affect and warmth.

Head nods. Another kinesic behavior that communicates immediacy is head nodding, particularly when head nods are used by a listener to respond to a speaker (Dittmann 1972). It is believed that in both primates and human beings, head nods originated as ritual bowing gestures which signal submission and friendliness (Eibl-Eibesfeldt 1974). This research indicated that head nods tended to be used to increase communication or friendliness and tended to be just the opposite of threat or dominance displays. When Rosenfeld (1966a, 1966b) asked subjects to simulate approval-seeking behaviors, the subjects nodded more frequently. Rosenfeld also found that head nods were reciprocated by two communicators, particularly as they became more familiar with one another. Finally, in several studies (Mehrabian 1971b; Mehrabian & Ksionzky 1972) of waiting-room situations, strangers communicated affiliativeness by increasing the number of positive head nods. Head nods are used by effective classroom teachers to communicate immediacy and to provide reinforcement to students. These nods also provide a student with feedback that the teacher is listening to and understanding their communication.

Open body positions. Several studies have found open body positions to communicate increased warmth or immediacy. Mehrabian (1969) found that female communicators using more open arm and leg positions communicated a more positive attitude. In a study of married couples, Beier and Sternberg (1977) found that "close" couples who reported less conflict and disagreement used more open leg positions than couples experiencing conflict. Evidently, folding one's arms and holding one's legs tightly together communicate defensiveness and coldness rather than immediacy. Teachers who maintain closed body positions are perceived as cold, unfriendly, and not very responsive to communication.

Bodily relaxation. Body relaxation communicates immediacy by demonstrating freedom from stress and anxiety. Tension is perceived negatively by interactants, since it communicates uncomfortable, anxious states and may be perceived as a buildup to an aggressive release of tension (Eibl-Eibesfeldt 1974). Indeed, Reece and Whitman (1961) found that an important part of therapist warmth includes using behaviors which are nonaggressive in nature. Relaxation has been identified by many researchers as an important part of being an immediate communicator. Reece and Whitman (1962) operationalized warmth as opposed to coldness by using four behaviors, one of which was "still, relaxed hands" versus "drumming the fingers." Mehrabian (1968a) included relaxed postures as an important component of immediacy. In a series of factor-analytic studies, Andersen, Andersen, and Jensen (1979) found that more relaxation and less tension were part of a perceived immediacy dimension. Mehrabian (1968b, 1969) found that relaxed rather than tense body positions communicated more liking and positive attitudes between two persons. LaFrance (1972) showed that posture sharing (the extent to which teachers and students assume symmetrical body positions) had a positive effect on rapport and student liking for their teacher. In a teaching context, Andersen (1979) found that more immediate teachers demonstrate more relaxed body postures. Evidently, teachers who are tense and anxious communicate negative attitudes to their pupils and are perceived as cold and nonimmediate.

Gestural behavior. Finally, kinesic immediacy is communicated through more gestural activity. Rosenfeld (1966a, 1966b) had people simulate approval-seeking behaviors. These people employed more overall gestural activity when seeking approval from others than at other times. Mehrabian and Williams (1969) found that when females used more gestures, they were perceived by others as more persuasive and felt that they were more persuasive. In a study of affiliative behavior, Mehrabian (1971b) found that more hand and arm gestures per minute were a part of communicating greater affiliation with others. Andersen, Andersen, and Jensen (1979) found that more overall bodily movement was part of perceived immediacy. Andersen (1979) found that more immediate college teachers employed more overall bodily movement. Gestures communicate interest and warmth, both in interpersonal interactions and while teaching. Gestures not only help to illustrate ideas but convey more warmth and enthusiasm for teaching.

Oculesics

The study of messages sent by the eyes is called oculesics. Eye contact is an invitation to communicate and a powerful immediacy cue. Communicators spend a large percentage of time looking at one another in both interpersonal and teaching contexts. Numerous researchers have shown eye contact and gaze to be an important component of immediacy. Argyle (1972) found that perceptions of intimacy were, in part, a function of increased eye contact. Recently, Andersen, Andersen, and Jensen (1979) found that more eye contact is an important part of both interpersonal immediacy and teacher immediacy. Eye contact performs an important monitoring function which communicates to another person that you are "taking account of them" (Kendon 1967). This monitoring function of eye contact signals availability for communication. Exline and Fehr (1978) explains that eye contact is a necessary behavior in communicating involvement. They maintain that absence of much visual attention is perceived as unwillingness to become involved with another. Similarly, Goffman (1964) maintains that eye contact is an important indicator of social accessibility.

Positive effects of eye contact.   Many studies indicate the positive interpersonal effects of eye contact. Goldberg, Kiesler, and Collins (1969) found that persons who spent more time gazing at an interviewer received higher socioemotional evaluations. In a study by Coutts and Schneider (1976), it was reported that friends engaged in longer and more frequent individual gaze and mutual gaze than did strangers. Beier and Sternberg's (1977) study of married couples reported that couples who experienced less conflict and disagreement looked at one another more frequently and for longer time periods. When Mehrabian and Friar (1969) asked experimental subjects to role-play liking for another person, they used substantially more eye contact. In a series of studies, increased eye contact was found to communicate a more positive attitude and increased affiliative behavior (Mehrabian 1968b, 1970, 1971b). Reece and Whitman (1961) found that therapist warmth was related to more glances at patients. Recently, Andersen (1979) found eye contact to be an important part of teacher warmth and immediacy.

Teacher eye contact.   Teachers who use more eye contact can more easily monitor and regulate their classes, and they also communicate more warmth and involvement to their students. Increased eye contact increases the opportunity for communication to occur and enables the teacher to respond to the many nonverbal behaviors of students. Teachers should position themselves so that they can and do establish eye contact with every student in the class. It is probable that immediacy cannot be successfully communicated by a teacher in the absence of eye contact.

Classroom Environment

Immediacy can be communicated by the physical environment of the classroom as well as by the body movements of the teacher. Classrooms which are clean, bright, attractive, and functional communicate immediacy. Moreover, classrooms which reduce physical barriers to communication make immediate interaction more probable.

Objects as barriers.   As Knapp (1972) indicates, most classrooms have a desk separating the students and their teachers. Several studies suggest that such physical barriers become psychological barriers as well. A study of doctors by White (1953) indicated that when a desk separated doctors and patients, only 10 percent of the patients were "at ease," whereas when the desk was removed, the number of "at ease" persons jumped to 55 percent. Mehrabian (1971a) and others have labeled environments which separate communicators as sociofugal and environments which bring communicators together as sociopetal. Sommer (1974, pp. 81–84) provides a good discussion of sociofugal classrooms, which include fixed seating in rows, teachers hidden behind podiums, and hard chairs for students. Similarly, Sommer (1974, p. 87) summarizes results which show participation increased in smaller classes. Teachers who want to convey warmth and immediacy must ascertain if the classroom has physical barriers which become psychological barriers and reduce communication.

Classroom arrangement.   Both Sommer (1974) and Adams (1969) indicate that students who are seated in the front row get the most attention and have the greatest opportunity to communicate with the teacher. Specifically, Adams (1969) reported that the greatest percentage and duration of communication came from the front row and middle tier of the classroom. Students in the front create a barrier between the teacher and students in the back. Teachers should consider arrangements that reduce the number of students who are behind other students. Hurt, Scott, and McCroskey (1978, pp. 92–99) provide a number of helpful suggestions on how to set up alternative seating arrangements in the classroom. Teachers should also move around the classroom to establish proxemic, oculesic, and haptic immediacy with *all* of their students. Typically, only students in close proximity to their teacher receive such immediacy. Finally, research shows that well-decorated, attractive classrooms convey more warmth and excitement to students (Sommer 1974, p. 95). A drab, depressing classroom will probably suppress many immediacy behaviors on the part of both students and teachers. Readers who are interested in a more detailed discussion of classroom environmental variables, including space, time, sound, color, lighting and artifacts, should read the essay by William Todd-Mancillas in this volume.

Chronemics

Chronemics is the study of time and what it communicates to other persons. Time is viewed as a commodity in America. In our rhetoric, time is spoken of as being wasted, saved, spent, and used, much as if it were money, food, or some other valuable resource. Spending time with someone communicates closer psychological distance, more availability, and mutuality of communication. In short, spending time with someone is an immediacy behavior. Mehrabian (1967) indicates that an important part of immediacy is use of time. He maintains that communication which is ongoing rather than past or present is more immediate.

Similarly, spending a greater duration of time with someone communicates more immediacy. Andersen, Andersen, and Jensen (1979) found that spending more time with someone was a component of communicated immediacy.

Arriving late probably communicates less immediacy as well. Baxter and Ward (1975) found secretaries considered late arrivers to be incompetent, lacking in composure, and communicating less friendliness and sociability. Similarly, teachers who arrive late or spend little time with students are increasing psychological distance and decreasing immediacy. A teacher's time is a scarce and valuable commodity for students in this culture. Certainly teacher availability is important in communicating immediacy.

MEASURING NONVERBAL IMMEDIACY

Most of the research findings on immediacy are conclusions from studies where one or two immediacy behaviors were manipulated and the resulting effects were measured. In most of these studies, immediacy levels were not measured, for it was simply assumed that increasing or decreasing a particular immediacy behavior would alter overall immediacy. There have been, however, a few efforts to directly measure the amount of immediacy present in an interaction, and these will be discussed.

There are at least three possible approaches toward measuring overall immediacy levels. First, one can utilize trained observers to count or code individual nonverbal behaviors previously conceptualized as indicating immediacy. For example, one could record the percentage of eye contact, the spatial distance between interactants, the number of smiles or head nods, and so on. Then various combinations of these behavioral observations could be used to indicate the amount of overall immediacy.

Second, immediacy can be measured by having trained observers, or the interactants themselves, record their perceptions of the extent to which each immediacy behavior is manifested. The person recording their perception of immediacy would respond to a set of scales which measure their overall perception of each immediacy behavior. The scales can be used to measure the degree of each immediacy behavior by the recorder.

Third, immediacy can be measured as a subjective gestalt or holistic impression without reference to particular behaviors. In this case, either trained observers or the actual interactants can be given scales to assess the overall immediacy of an interaction. The scales would assess the overall warmth, closeness, intimacy, or immediacy without reference to the behaviors used to communicate these impressions.

Scales designed to assess immediacy through the second and third methods are available in an article by Andersen, Andersen, and Jensen (1979). The first method has received less attention, but Feldman and Lobato-Barrera (1979) counted and recorded four behaviors as indicating overall immediacy levels. These methods suggest that immediacy can be measured by a trained observer who is not a participant in the interaction as well as by people involved in the interaction. The first method discussed, counting and coding individual immediacy behaviors, necessitates a trained outside observer. People involved in an interaction simply cannot simultaneously count and code behaviors and also interact. The second and third methods, however, do not necessitate using an outside observer. People involved in interactions can and do form overall impressions of immediacy as well as the extent to which individual immediacy behaviors are manifested. Andersen (1979) found that outside observers' and interactants' perceptions of the immediacy behaviors manifested correlated highly (.80). Andersen (1979) also found that perceptions of individual immediacy behaviors manifested and overall perceptions of immediacy correlated moderately well (.67). What still needs to be researched, however, is the extent to which people's perceptions of immediacy correlate with the first method, where an actual count of immediacy behaviors is made.

TEACHER IMMEDIACY AND LEARNING

What is the relationship of teacher immediacy to student learning? Generally, the results of empirical studies support the position that teacher immediacy has a positive impact on student learning, particularly on affective outcomes. In this section, the impact of teacher immediacy on each of the three domains of learning will be discussed.

Immediacy and Affective Learning

It is well established in the study of interpersonal communication contexts that immediacy behaviors communicate feelings of warmth and positive affect and engender feelings of interpersonal attraction (see Jensen & Andersen 1979; Mehrabian 1971a). This finding has received some support in instructional communication contexts as well. Of the three domains of learning, immediacy behaviors have their most powerful impact on affective learning.

Students feel more positive affect for immediate teachers. In fact, half of the variance in college student liking for an instructor could be accounted for by immediacy behaviors of the teacher (Andersen 1979). A study of college student preferences for teacher-pupil interaction patterns indicated that responding warmly to students was a major characteristic of an ideal teacher (Hyman 1968). Beck and Lambert (1977) observed that college students responded very negatively to a formal, nonimmediate instructor. In fact, simply telling a college class that their substitute teacher was known as warm (as opposed to cold) produced higher evaluations for the substitute instructor. Sixth graders also viewed teacher warmth and friendliness as a critical component of teacher effectiveness. Kindergarten teachers who smile more are perceived as more effective (Harrington 1955). In studies of elementary schoolchildren, Ryans (1960, 1964) found teacher warmth and friendliness to be important predictors of positive student response, but he also found these characteristics to be less important on the secondary level. Across many grade levels, Leeds (1950) observed that creating a friendly atmosphere was one of the two most important elements in establishing good teacher-student relationships.

Immediate teachers also produce more student affect toward the subject matter and school in general. Robert (1973) suggests that general student apathy might be reduced by teachers engaging in behaviors that are immediate. Andersen (1979) found that more positive student attitudes toward the subject matter content and toward the course in general were positively correlated with increases in college teachers' immediacy levels.

Immediacy and Higher-Order Affective Responses

Teacher immediacy is associated with a second set of learning consequences, which are higher-order affective outcomes. These outcomes are behaviorally manifested and have sometimes been discussed as a separate learning domain (cf. Andersen 1979; Nussbaum & Scott 1979). If treated as a separate category, behaviorally manifested affective outcomes should not be confused as representing Bloom, Englehart, Furst, Hill, and Krathwohl's (1956) psychomotor domain.[1]

One behaviorally manifested affective outcome of immediacy is increased student participation in class. A variety of experimental studies have consistently supported the finding that subjects in conditions with more immediate interactants are more likely to engage in greater amounts of verbal interaction (Kleinke, Staneski, & Berger 1975; Krail & Leventhal 1976; McDowell 1973; Mehrabian 1971b; Reece & Whitman 1962). Siegman (1978) reports that people interacting with a warm person as opposed to a cold person engaged in fewer and/or shorter silent pauses. However, in a series of studies relating verbal productivity to therapist warmth, Siegman (1978) generally failed to find a relationship between verbal productivity or output and therapist warmth. In a classroom study, Kelley (1950) found that instructor warmth increased student interaction. When college students were given a description of an instructor, 56 percent of

---

[1] The psychomotor domain is narrowly confined to describe those learning activities which involve neuromuscular coordination through the manipulation of objects or materials. Krathwohl, Bloom, and Masia (1964) report that there are few psychomotor objectives utilized, and most relate to handwriting, physical education, and the physiological production of speech. The psychomotor domain is not discussed in this section because immediacy variables presently seem irrelevant to psychomotor outcomes. Immediacy may affect the drive to engage in psychomotor activities, but this would then be treated as a behaviorally manifested affective outcome.

the students initiated interaction with the instructor when he was described as warm, while only 32 percent initiated interaction when the instructor was described as cold.

Second, students are also more likely to engage in continued reading and studying when the teacher is immediate. Cogan (1958, 1963) reports a strong relationship for secondary school students between affiliative behaviors of teachers and self-initiated work by students. Furthermore, college students are more likely to voluntarily enroll in future classes in the same subject area when the instructor is immediate (Andersen 1979). Beck and Lambert (1977) found a greater percentage of students interested in dropping a class after a class session with an instructor who was formal and nonimmediate.

A third behaviorally manifested affective result of increased immediacy is the greater persuasive power of the teacher. Students of immediate teachers are more willing to engage in the actions suggested by the content. In the interpersonal context, Mehrabian and Williams (1969) found that both intended persuasiveness and perceived persuasiveness were associated with greater immediacy. Andersen (1979) found that students of more immediate teachers are more willing to engage in the communication strategies suggested in the course.

Immediacy and Cognitive Learning

The effects of immediacy on the cognitive domain of learning are less clear and less positive. There are a few studies which support positive effects on cognitive learning for some immediacy variables. For example, Breed, Christiansen, and Larson (1972) found that students who received eye contact from the lecturer had increased lecture comprehension. Coats and Smidchens (1966) found that speaker dynamism and information recall by students were significantly related. A dynamic speaker was one who used vocal inflection, gestures, eye contact, and a high level of overall animation. Gauger's (1952) results also support this relationship in that eleventh and twelth grade students scored higher on a listening comprehension test if they heard a lecture accompanied by gestures rather than one without gestures. Kleinfeld (1973) used close proximity, frequent smiling, and touch in a one-to-one counseling session and found that these variables increased learning for Eskimo students. A recent study by Esp (1978) found that positive rather than negative kinesic behavior had a positive effect on student learning but only if the teacher was female.

Several researchers, however, have failed to substantiate a relationship between immediacy and short-term cognitive learning. Andersen (1979) and Gardner and Andersen (1980) found no evidence to support a relationship between teacher immediacy and student short-term cognitive learning.

Examining long-term cognitive gains, Christiansen (1960) found a relationship between teacher warmth and vocabulary achievement and arithmetic achievement of fourth and fifth graders. Harrington (1955) found that smiling kindergarten teachers were associated with pupil growth on that level. Medley and Mitzel (1958), however, found no effect for teacher warmth on the intellectual growth of pupils.

Thus, the effects of teacher immediacy on student cognitive learning are less positive. Research supports a consistent and somewhat powerful effect for immediacy in influencing the affective domain at all levels. In terms of cognitive learning, to the extent that affective learning positively influences cognitive achievement, immediacy probably has positive effects on cognitive learning. To the extent that cognitive learning is influenced by other factors, such as student intelligence, background, subject matter motivation, and so on, immediacy has little if any effects on cognitive learning.

In summary, a rather substantial argument can be made for the influence of teacher immediacy on affective learning outcomes. There may be some influence of teacher immediacy on student cognitive learning, but these effects are less direct and less certain. Yet even if immediacy had no positive effects on cognitive learning, its importance in affective outcomes together with the importance of affective outcomes in the educational process makes teacher immediacy an important part of effective teaching.

Changing Your Immediacy Level— Some Cautions

Theory and research on the immediacy construct suggest that it is a positive force in the classroom, particularly in terms of producing better teacher-student relationships. However, before a teacher attempts to increase his or her immediacy level, a few cautions should be noted. First, immediacy should not be confused with extreme intimacy. Although the terms *immediacy* and *intimacy* have been used interchangeably by a number of researchers (Argyle 1972; Patterson 1973, 1978a, 1978b), it may be time to separate the two conceptually. The term *intimacy* has connotations of extreme interpersonal warmth and closeness. It is our position that immediacy can be manifested at any stage of a relationship, even when you first meet someone. Intimacy is typically engaged in only in long-term relationships which are characterized by high degrees of acquaintance and trust. The term *intimacy,* as used in this chapter, is therefore equivalent to extremes in immediacy. For example, a pat on the arm or shoulder would be an immediacy behavior, while a pat on the upper, inner thigh would be an intimacy behavior in most relationships.

It is possible, however, for a true immediacy behavior to be *perceived* as an intimacy behavior. If this happens, some classroom problems might arise for the immediate teacher. Junior high and secondary teachers should be especially alert for possible misinterpretation of these behaviors. Teachers should engage in immediacy behaviors that will not be misinterpreted as intimate or sexual behavior. Misinterpretations will also be less likely if immediacy behaviors are part of the teacher's interaction pattern with everyone in the classroom. Being immediate only to opposite-sex students or to a teacher's favorite students can lead to misinterpretations of intimacy and should be avoided.

A second caution is that teacher immediacy cues are probably perceived positively only if student attitudes toward the teacher are neutral or positive. The use of immediacy cues by a teacher who is perceived negatively by students may produce an equilibrium or avoidance response; thus actually increasing the psychological distance between teachers and students. Among strangers, increases in immediacy by one person will result in compensatory decreases in immediacy by the other person in an effort to maintain equilibrium (Patterson 1973). So, teachers should ascertain whether students are reciprocating their immediacy cues, an indication of a positive response. If students are using equilibrium behaviors (that is, turning away, backing up, reducing eye contact), the teacher is premature in establishing such a high level of immediacy.

Finally, since there are a variety of ways to be immediate, teachers can select those immediacy behaviors with which they feel most comfortable and avoid those immediacy behaviors that create personal discomfort. If teachers are having problems with being perceived as too immediate or intimate, they can reduce their overall amount of immediacy, or they can substitute immediacy behaviors which are less likely to be misinterpreted. On the other hand, if teachers are perceived as cold, distant, or aloof, they can increase their overall immediacy by consciously engaging in more immediacy behaviors. However, teachers who genuinely feel cold, distant, and negative toward their students will have difficulty communicating genuine warmth and immediacy. While feigning immediacy may fool some students, considerable nonverbal research indicates that true feeling "leaks" to receivers in a number of ways (cf. Mehrabian 1971a). A genuinely warm, positive attitude toward students is probably a prerequisite for a teacher to successfully communicate immediacy.

It is interesting to note, however, that some teachers who have been trained to be more immediate often begin to *feel* more warmth and closeness to their students. These reports are consistent with the position of Bem (1970) and the radical behaviorist school, who have shown that attitudes often change in response to changes in behavior. Collins (1976) found that teachers trained to be more enthusiastic developed more enthusiastic attitudes toward teaching. Some teachers who want to be warm and immediate have trouble communicating these feelings to their students. These teachers may profit from learning the specific behaviors which communicate immediacy to their students.

Thus, teacher immediacy behaviors have the potential to make the teacher and the learning environment more attractive to the student and to positively influence the quality of classroom interaction. This chapter suggests behaviors which teachers might employ to communicate a message of immediacy and thus of warmth, friendship, and interpersonal closeness.

SUMMARY

This chapter provides an examination of the impact of teacher nonverbal immediacy behaviors on classroom instruction. The chapter begins with a discussion of the three learning domains (cognitive, affective, and psychomotor) and suggests that greater attention should be given to methods of increasing learning in the affective domain. Teacher communication of immediacy through nonverbal behaviors is suggested as an important way to positively influence the affective domain.

Nonverbal immediacy behaviors are approach behaviors which signal availability for communication and create increased sensory stimulation. Immediacy behaviors communicate interpersonal closeness and warmth.

Seven codes of nonverbal communication are specifically discussed as potentially communicating nonverbal immediacy. Under proxemics, the study of the use of interpersonal space and distance, the teacher's physical distance in the classroom, and body angle and orientation are immediacy cues. Touch, or haptics, is a second immediacy behavior discussed. Third, vocalics, or the nonverbal elements of the human voice, are discussed as immediacy indicators. Communication through body movement, or kinesics, is a fourth area for communicating immediacy. Smiling, head nods, open body positions, bodily relaxation, and gestural activity are included in this topic. Eye behavior, or oculesics, is a fifth important way by which immediacy can be communicated. Sixth, the classroom environment itself, including classroom decoration and arrangements and seating patterns, is an area of immediacy communication. Finally, chronemics, or the study of time, is discussed as another nonverbal area from which immediacy messages are likely to originate.

Next, three possible approaches for measuring nonverbal immediacy are discussed and compared. Possible methods include using behavioral reports or counts by trained raters, using perceptual measures of individual immediacy behaviors, and/or using subjective gestalt measures of overall immediacy.

The final section of the chapter examines the empirical research findings linking teacher immediacy to learning outcomes. Research findings support a relationship between teacher immediacy and affective learning outcomes. Attitudes toward the teacher and toward the subject matter are influenced by immediacy. Higher-order affective responses or behavioral outcomes such as increased interaction and greater influence are also related to instructor immediacy. Cognitive learning seems less influenced by immediacy behaviors. The chapter concludes with some cautions about potential dangers of immediacy behavior, particularly in terms of potential confusion with intimacy. Some guidelines for the classroom instructor are suggested in choosing appropriate immediate behaviors.

SUGGESTED READINGS

HURT, H. T., M. D. SCOTT, and J. C. McCROSKEY. *Communication in the Classroom*. Reading, Mass.: Addison-Wesley Publishing Co., Inc., 1978.

This is probably the most useful single book for classroom teachers interested in communication. Its strengths include a solid research foundation, good breadth, and an easy, readable style. It includes an entire chapter on nonverbal communication.

KIBLER, R. J., L. L. BARKER, and D. T. MILES. *Behavioral Objectives and Instruction*. Boston: Allyn & Bacon, Inc., 1970.

This book is an excellent pioneering effort to relate Bloom's taxonomy to the classroom. It has a pragmatic focus designed to be used by classroom teachers in instructional development.

MEHRABIAN, A. *Silent Messages*. Belmont, Calif.: Wadsworth Publishing Co. Inc., 1971.

Mehrabian provides one of the first and best overviews of many of the important functions of nonverbal communication. Included is an excellent overview of both verbal and nonverbal immediacy.

NIMMO, D. (ed.) *Communication Yearbook 3*. New Brunswick, N.J.: Transaction Books, 1979.

The communication yearbook provides the reader with the best research of the International Communication Association and topical overviews of theory and research. The instructional communication chapters are particularly relevant to readers of this book. Among them is Janis Andersen's empirical study of immediacy and college teaching effectiveness.

SIEGMAN, A. W., and S. FELDSTEIN, (eds.) *Nonverbal Behavior and Communication*. New York: John Wiley & Sons, Inc., 1978.

This is an excellent overview of many important areas of nonverbal research written by some of the outstanding researchers in the field. This book is a must for students of nonverbal communication.

REFERENCES

ADAMS, R. S. "Location as a feature of instructional interaction." *Merrill-Palmer Quarterly*, 1969, *15*, 309–21.

ANDERSEN, J. F. "The relationship between teacher immediacy and teaching effectiveness." In D. Nimmo (ed.), *Communication Yearbook 3*. New Brunswick, N.J.: Transaction Books, 1979.

ANDERSEN, J. F., P. A. ANDERSEN, and A. D. JENSEN. "The Measurement of nonverbal immediacy." *Journal of Applied Communication Research*, 1979, *7*, 153–80.

ANDERSEN, P. A., and K. LEIBOWITZ. "The development and nature of the construct touch avoidance." *Environmental Psychology and Nonverbal Behavior*, 1978, *3*, 89–106.

ARGYLE, M. *The Psychology of Interpersonal Behaviour* (2nd ed.). London: Penguin Books, 1972.

BARR, A. S. *Characteristic Differences in the Teaching Performance of Good and Poor Teachers of the Social Studies*. Bloomington, Ill.: Public School Publishing Company, 1929.

BASSETT, R. E., and M. J. SMYTHE. *Communication and Instruction*. New York: Harper & Row Publishers, Inc., 1979.

BAXTER, L., and J. WARD. "Newsline." *Psychology Today*, 1975, *8* (8), 28.

BECK, W. W., and G. E. LAMBERT. "First impressions and classroom climate." *Kappa Delta Pi Record*, 1977, *13* (4), 121-22.

BEIER, E. G., and D. P. STERNBERG. "Marital communication: Subtle cues between newlyweds." *Journal of Communication*, 1977, *27*, 92-97.

BEM, D. J. *Beliefs, Attitudes, and Human Affairs*. Monterey, Calif.: Brooks/ Cole Publishing Co., 1970.

BLOOM, B. S. (ed.) *A Taxonomy of Educational Objectives, Handbook I: The Cognitive Domain*. New York: Longmans, Green Company, 1956.

BREED, G., E. CHRISTIANSEN, and D. LARSON. "Effect of a lecturer's gaze direction upon teaching effectiveness." *Catalog of Selected Documents in Psychology*, 1972, *2*, 115.

BROWN, R. *Social Psychology*. New York: The Free Press, 1965.

CHRISTIANSEN, C. M. "Relationships between pupil achievement, pupil affect-need, teacher warmth, and teacher permissiveness. *Journal of Educational Psychology*, 1960, *51*, 169-74.

COATS, W. D., and U. SMIDCHENS. "Audience recall as a function of speaker dynamism." *Journal of Educational Psychology*, 1966, *57*, 189-91.

COGAN, M. L. "The behavior of teachers and the productive behavior of their pupils." *Journal of Experimental Education*, 1958, *27*, 89-124.

COGAN, M. L. "Research on the behavior of teachers: A new phase." *Journal of Teaching Education*, 1963, *14*, 238-43.

COLLINS, M. L. *The Effects of Training for Enthusiasm on the Enthusiasm Displayed by Preservice Elementary Teachers*. 1976. (ERIC Document No. ED-130-337).

COUTTS, L. M., and F. W. SCHNEIDER. "Affiliative conflict theory: An investigation of intimacy equilibrium and compensation hypothesis." *Journal of Personality and Social Psychology*, 1976, *34*, 135-42.

DITTMANN, A. T. "Developmental factors in conversational behavior." *Journal of Communication*, 1972, *22*, 404-23.

EIBL-EIBESFELDT, I. *Love and Hate: The Natural History of Behavior Patterns*. New York: Schocken Books, 1974.

ESP, B. A. "The effects of teacher kinesic communication upon student learning and attitudes." *Dissertation Abstracts International*, 1978, *39* (5-A), 2828.

EXLINE, R. V., and B. J. FEHR. "Applications of semiosis to the study of visual interaction." In A. W. Siegman and S. Feldstein (eds.), *Nonverbal Behavior and Communication*. Hillsdale, N.J.: Lawrence Erlbaum Associates, 1978.

EXLINE, R. V., and L. C. WINTERS. "Affective relations and mutual glances in dyads." In S. Tomkins and C. Izzard (eds.), *Affect, Cognition, and Personality*. New York: Springer Publishing Co., 1965.

FELDMAN, R. S. and D. LOBATO-BARRERA. "Attitudes, cognition, and nonverbal communicative behavior." Paper presented to the annual conference of the American Educational Research Association, San Francisco, April, 1979.

GARDNER, J., and J. F. ANDERSEN. "The impact of lecturer nonverbal expressiveness on improving mediated instruction." Paper presented to the Eastern Communication Association, Ocean City, Maryland, 1980.

GAUGER, P. W. "The effect of gesture and the presence or absence of speaking on listening comprehension of eleventh and twelfth grade high school pupils." Cited in C. W. Dow (ed.), Abstracts of theses in the field of speech and drama. *Speech Monographs,* 1952, *19,* 116–17.

GOFFMAN, E. *Behavior in Public Places.* Glencoe, Ill.: The Free Press, 1964.

GOLDBERG, G. N., G. A. KIESLER, and B. E. COLLINS. "Visual behavior and face-to-face distance interaction." *Sociometry,* 1969, *32,* 43–53.

GUTSELL, L. M., and J. F. ANDERSEN. "Perceptual and behavioral responses to smiling." Paper presented to the International Communication Association, Acapulco, Mexico, 1980.

HARPER, R. G., A. N. WIENS, and J. D. MATARAZZO. *Nonverbal Communication: The State of the Art.* New York: John Wiley & Sons, Inc., 1968.

HARRINGTON, G. M. "Smiling as a measure of teacher effectiveness." *Journal of Educational Research,* 1955, *48,* 715–17.

HURT, H. T., M. D. SCOTT, and J. C. McCROSKEY. *Communication in the Classroom.* Reading, Mass.: Addison-Wesley Publishing Co., Inc., 1978.

HYMAN, R. T. "The concept of an ideal teacher/student relationship: A comparison and critique." In R. T. Hyman (ed.), *Teaching: A Vantage Point for Study.* New York: J. B. Lippincott Company, 1968.

JENSEN, A. D., and P. A. ANDERSEN. "The relationship among communication traits, communication behaviors, and interpersonal perception variables." Paper presented to the International Communication Association, Philadelphia, Pa., 1979.

KELLEY, H. H. "The warm-cold variable in first impressions of persons." *Journal of Personality,* 1950, *18,* 431–39.

KENDON, A. "Some functions of gaze direction in social interaction." *Acta Psychologica,* 1967, *26,* 22–63.

KIBLER, R. J., L. L. BARKER, and D. T. MILES. *Behavioral Objectives and Instruction.* Boston: Allyn & Bacon, Inc., 1970.

KLEINFELD, J. *Using Nonverbal Warmth to Increase Learning: A Cross-Cultural Experiment.* Fairbanks, Alaska: University of Alaska, 1973. (ERIC Document No. ED-081-568).

KLEINKE, C. L., R. A. STANESKI, and D. E. BERGER. "Evaluation of an interviewer as a function of interviewer gaze, reinforcement of subject gaze, and interviewer attractiveness." *Journal of Personality and Social Psychology,* 1975, *31,* 115–22.

KNAPP, M. L. *Nonverbal Communication in Human Interaction.* New York: Holt, Rinehart & Winston, 1972.

KRAIL, K. A., and G. LEVENTHAL. The sex variable in intrusion of personal space. *Sociometry,* 1976, *39,* 170–73.

KRATHWOHL, D. R., B. S. BLOOM, and B. MASIA. *A Taxonomy of Educational Objectives, Handbook II: The Affective Domain.* New York: David McKay Co., Inc., 1964.

LaFRANCE, M. "Nonverbal synchrony and rapport: Analysis by the cross-lag panel technique." *Social Psychology Quarterly,* 1972, *42,* 66–70.

LEEDS, C. H. "A scale for measuring teacher-pupil attitudes and teacher-pupil rapport." *Psychological Monographs,* 1950, *64* (6).

McDOWELL, K. V. "Accommodations of verbal and nonverbal behaviors as a function of the manipulation of interaction distance and eye contact." *Proceedings of the Eighty-First Annual Convention of the American Psychological Association,* 1973, *8,* 207-8.

MEDLEY, D. M., and H. E. MITZEL. "A technique for measuring classroom behavior." *Journal of Educational Psychology,* 1958, *49,* 86-92.

MEHRABIAN, A. "Orientation behaviors and nonverbal attitude in communicators." *Journal of Communication,* 1967, *17,* 324-32.

MEHRABIAN, A. "Inference of attitude from the posture, orientation, and distance of a communicator." *Journal of Consulting and Clinical Psychology,* 1968a, *32,* 296-308.

MEHRABIAN, A. "Relationship of attitude to seating, posture, orientation, and distance." *Journal of Personality and Social Psychology,* 1968b, *10,* 26-30.

MEHRABIAN, A. Significance of posture and position in the communication of attitude and status relationships. *Psychological Bulletin,* 1969, *71,* 359-72.

MEHRABIAN, A. "The development and validation of measures of affiliative tendency and sensitivity to rejection." *Educational and Psychological Measurement,* 1970, *30,* 417-28.

MEHRABIAN, A. *Silent Messages.* Belmont, Calif.: Wadsworth Publishing Co., Inc., 1971a.

MEHRABIAN, A. "Verbal and nonverbal interaction of strangers in a waiting situation." *Journal of Experimental Research in Personality,* 1971b, *5,* 127-38.

MEHRABIAN, A., and S. R. FERRIS. "Inference of attitudes from nonverbal communication in two channels." *Journal of Consulting Psychology,* 1967, *31,* 248-53.

MEHRABIAN, A., and J. J. FRIAR. "Encoding of attitude by a seated communicator via posture and position cues." *Journal of Consulting and Clinical Psychology,* 1969, *33,* 330-36.

MEHRABIAN, A., and S. KSIONZKY. "Models for affiliative and conformity behavior." *Psychological Bulletin,* 1970, *74,* 110-26.

MEHRABIAN, A., and S. KSIONZKY. "Categories of social behavior." *Comparative Group Studies,* 1972, *3,* 425-36.

MEHRABIAN, A., and M. WILLIAMS. "Nonverbal concomitants of perceived and intended persuasiveness." *Journal of Personality and Social Psychology,* 1969, *13,* 37-58.

MONTAGUE, A. *Touching: The Human Significance of the Skin.* New York: Columbia University Press, 1970.

MORRIS, D. *Intimate Behavior.* New York: Random House, Inc., 1971.

NUSSBAUM, J. F., and M. D. SCOTT. "Instructor communication behaviors and their relationship to classroom learning." In D. Nimmo (eds.), *Communication Yearbook 3.* New Brunswick, N.J.: Transaction Books, 1979.

PATTERSON, M. L. "Compensation in nonverbal immediacy behaviors: A review." *Sociometry,* 1973, *36* (2), 237-52.

PATTERSON, M. L. "Interpersonal distance, affect, and equilibrium theory." *Journal of Social Psychology,* 1977, *101,* 205-14.

PATTERSON, M. L. "Arousal change and cognitive labeling: Pursuing the mediators of intimacy exchange." *Environmental Psychology and Nonverbal Behavior,* 1968a, *3,* 17-22.

PATTERSON, M. L. "Nonverbal intimacy exchange: Problems and prospects."

Paper presented to the Second National Conference on Body Language, New York, 1978b.

REECE, M. M., and R. N. WHITMAN. "Warmth and expressive movements." *Psychological Reports,* 1961, *8,* 76.

REECE, M. M., and R. N. WHITMAN. "Expressive movements, warmth, and verbal reinforcement." *Journal of Abnormal and Social Psychology,* 1962, *64,* 234–36.

ROBERT, M. *Loneliness in the Schools.* Niles, Ill.: Argus Communications, 1973.

ROSENFELD, H. M. "Approval-seeking and approval-inducing functions of verbal and nonverbal responses in the dyad." *Journal of Personality and Social Psychology,* 1966a, *4,* 597–605.

ROSENFELD, H. M. "Instrumental affiliative functions of facial and gestural expressions." *Journal of Personality and Social Psychology,* 1966b, *4,* 65-72.

ROSENFELD, H. M. "Nonverbal reciprocation of approval: An experimental analysis." *Journal of Experimental Social Psychology,* 1967, *3,* 102–11.

RYANS, D. G. *Characteristics of Teachers.* Washington, D.C.: American Council on Education, 1960.

RYANS, D. G. "Research on teacher behavior in the context of the teacher characteristics study." In B. J. Biddle and W. J. Ellena (eds.), *Contemporary Research on Teacher Effectiveness.* New York: Holt, Rinehart & Winston, 1964.

SCHERER, K. R. "Acoustic concomitants of emotional dimensions: Judging affect from synthesized tone sequences." In S. Weitz (ed.), *Nonverbal Communication* (2nd ed.). New York: Oxford University Press, 1979.

SCHUSLER, R. A. "Nonverbal communication in the elementary classroom." *Theory into Practice,* 1971, *10,* 282–89.

SIEGMAN, A. W. "The telltale voice: Nonverbal messages of verbal communication." In A. W. Siegman and S. Feldstein (eds.), *Nonverbal Behavior and Communication.* New York: John Wiley & Sons, Inc., 1978.

SOMMER, R. *Tight Spaces: Hard Architecture and How to Humanize It.* Englewood Cliffs, N.J.: Prentice-Hall, Inc., 1974.

THOMPSON, J. H. *Beyond Words: Nonverbal Communication in the Classroom.* New York: Citation Press, 1973.

TRAGER, G. L. "Paralanguage: A first approximation." *Studies in Linguistics,* 1958, *13,* 1–12.

WHITE, A. G. "The patient sits down: A clinical note." *Psychosomatic Medicine,* 1953, *15,* 256–57.

CHAPTER SEVEN
COMMUNICATION APPREHENSION IN THE CLASSROOM

Vicki S. Freimuth*

*Dr. Freimuth is Associate Professor, Department of Communication Arts and Theatre, at the University of Maryland.

NATURE OF THE PROBLEM

Education is a communication process. Students must use speaking, listening, and writing communication skills to receive instruction, clarify their understanding, and demonstrate learning. Yet, some students are handicapped in the classroom by severe anxiety about communicating.

But what, exactly, does it feel like to have this kind of anxiety. Shirley Radl (1976), a successful journalist and free-lance writer, describes her feelings.

> Having personally suffered from shyness in varying degrees nearly all of my life, I know full well how it got started—skinny, homely little kid, skinnier and homelier teenager—and know all too well that neither the shyness researchers or those I've interviewed exaggerated how really awful and crazy it feels. I have known what it is to no matter what the circumstance, feel self-conscious of my every gesture, have trouble swallowing and talking, see my hands tremble for no apparent reasons, feel as if I were freezing to death while perspiring profusely, be confused about issues I am thoroughly familiar with, and imagine all sorts of terrible things that might happen to me—the least of which being that I would lose my job for being a public disgrace.
>
> I have experienced dizzy spells and twitching when in the company of absolutely nonthreatening men, women, and children. I've known what it is to avoid going to the grocery store because I couldn't face the checker, to become excessively nervous while chatting with the man who delivers the milk, or be unable to tolerate the watchful gaze of my children's friends while making popcorn for them. I have known what it is to have the feeling that I was stumbling naked through life with the whole thing being broadcast internationally via Telstar. (p. 24)

Labels Used to Describe the Problem

Apprehension of speaking before others is a phenomenon with numerous labels. The early research labeled this apprehension "stage fright" and focused on the fear of public speaking. "Communication apprehension" (CA) is a label with a much broader meaning. McCroskey coined the term and defines it as

. . . a broad-based fear or anxiety related to the act of communication held by a large number of individuals. The individual high in this apprehension is a person for whom apprehension about participating in communication outweighs the projected gain from communicating in a given situation. He or she anticipates negative feelings and outcomes from communication, and will avoid communication if possible, or suffer from a variety of anxiety-type feelings when forced to communicate. (McCroskey & Daly 1976, p. 68)

Phillips (1977) labels the phenomenon "reticence" and describes the problems associated with it:

1. Inability to open conversations with strangers or to make small talk.
2. Inability to extend conversations or to initiate friendships.
3. Inability to follow the thread of discussion or to make pertinent remarks in discussion.
4. Inability to answer questions asked in a normal classroom or job situation.
5. Incompetence at answering questions that arise on the job or in the classroom, not through lack of knowledge but an ability to phrase or time answers.
6. Inability to deliver a complete message even though it is planned and organized.
7. General ineptitude in communication situations characterized by avoidance of participation. (p. 37)

Fear of oral communication is also labeled "speech anxiety" (Mulac & Sherman 1974), "unwillingness to communicate" (Burgoon 1976) and "shyness" (Zimbardo 1977).

State versus Trait Communication Apprehension

This chapter will focus on CA viewed as trait rather than state apprehension. Spielberger (1966) and Lamb (1972) have made a distinction between two types of apprehension. First, apprehension which is a function of a particular communication situation, such as giving a public speech or interviewing for a new job, is called "state" apprehension. "Trait" apprehension, on the other hand, is characterized by fear or anxiety with respect to many different communication situations. Thus, a person with high trait CA may be anxious about speaking to one other person as well as giving a public speech. Almost everyone experiences state CA when they perform before a large group, and this anxious reaction is considered normal. In fact, a national survey conducted by R. H. Bruskin Associates in 1973 revealed that 40 percent of the 2,543 adult respondents checked "speaking before a group" as one of their common fears.

Extent of the Problem

While fewer people have high levels of trait CA, the extent of the problem is far greater than many would suspect. Based on data from nearly twenty thousand college students at three universities over the past eight years, it is estimated that between 15 and 20 percent of American college students suffer from debilitating oral communication apprehension (McCroskey 1977).

Other Types of Communication Apprehension

Using oral communication apprehension as an analogue, Daly and Miller (1975) identified writing apprehension as a general anxiety about writing. They suggested that in classrooms, students with writing apprehension are individuals who consistently fail to turn in writing assignments, who do not attend class when writing is required, and who seldom voluntarily enroll in courses which demand writing (Daly & Miller 1975).

Another form of communication apprehension which can interfere with learning is receiver apprehension. Wheeless (1975) describes this as an apprehension about receiving information. He suggests that individuals with this form of apprehension may have difficulty processing information and adjusting psychologically to messages sent by others.

Even though much research has been conducted on CA, the uniqueness of the trait has been challenged. In a recent critique of CA, Porter (1979) has suggested that CA may be a subset of generalized anxiety and may not be the broad-based trait described in its definitions. Indeed, Porter contends that we may be giving new labels to the "old" public speaking anxiety.

DIAGNOSING THE COMMUNICATION APPREHENSIVE STUDENT

An introduction to the problem of CA usually prompts teachers to ask how one can tell if a student experiences high levels of apprehension. Traditionally, CA has been measured in three general domains: physiologically, behaviorally, and psychologically with self-report measures.

Physiological Measures

Physiological measures include monitoring such bodily reactions to stress as the change in heart rate while communicating and the degree of perspiration on the palms of the hands. Since such measures are time-consuming, costly, and quite obtrusive, they are of little use to classroom teachers for identifying high CA students.

Behavioral Measures

The second approach to measuring CA is with behavioral checklists. Generally, these checklists are used for assessing public communication behaviors and include such behaviors as lack of eye contact, trembling knees and hands, shuffling feet, heavy breathing, and repeated swallowing (Clevenger & King 1961). While such checklists might be useful in courses which include some public communication, most teachers will not find them too useful for identifying the high communication apprehensive students.

Psychological or Self-Report Measures

Several scales have been developed for the measurement of communication apprehension with the use of self-report measures. The simplest diagnostic tool available for oral communication apprehension is the *Personal Report of Communication Apprehension* (PRCA) which was developed by McCroskey (1970). The PRCA has been employed in numerous studies since 1970 and has consistently yielded realiability estimates above .90. A 1975 article (McCroskey 1975) summarizes the evidence of the validity of the scale (see figure 7-1 for a copy of the PRCA and instructions for scoring it). Garrison and Garrison (1977) have developed a scale, named the *Measure of Elementary Communication Apprehension* (MECA), which is designed to measure trait CA among preliterate children (see figure 7-2). A similar self-report measure was developed by Daly and Miller (1975) to measure writing apprehension, the *Writing Apprehension Test* (WAT) (see figure 7-3 for a copy of this scale), and by Wheeless (1975) to measure receiver apprehension, the *Receiver Apprehension Test* (RAT) (see figure 7-4).

Problems in Measurement

Two problems have plagued researchers attempting to measure CA. First, the three approaches to measuring CA have yielded low correlations. Two interpretations have been offered for these low correlations. Freimuth (1976) suggested a theoretical perspective for CA which illustrates this measurement problem. Prior to 1976, little effort had been made to examine CA in a broader theoretical framework. Even though in prior research the construct had been given labels such as stage fright, speech anxiety, and reticence, it had consistently been identified as an emotional state. Clevenger's (1955) early attempt to define stage fright led to the following conclusion:

> . . . It should be obvious that we are dealing with an emotion although considerable doubt exists as to the exact nature of that emotion. (Clevenger 1955 p. 28)

FIGURE 7-1 Personal Report of Communication Apprehension (PRCA)

Directions: This instrument is composed of twenty-five statements concerning feelings about communicating with other people. Please indicate the degree to which each statement applies to you by marking whether you (a) Strongly Agree, (2) Agree, (3) Are Undecided, (4) Disagree, or (5) Strongly Disagree with each statement. There are no right or wrong answers. Work quickly, just record your first impression.

		SA	A	UN	D	SD
1.	While participating in a conversation with a new acquaintance I feel very nervous.	1	2	3	4	5
2.	I have no fear of facing an audience.	1	2	3	4	5
3.	I talk less because I'm shy.	1	2	3	4	5
4.	I look forward to expressing my opinions at meetings.	1	2	3	4	5
5.	I am afraid to express myself in a group.	1	2	3	4	5
6.	I look forward to an opportunity to speak in public.	1	2	3	4	5
7.	I find the prospect of speaking mildly pleasant.	1	2	3	4	5
8.	When communicating, my posture feels strained and unnatural.	1	2	3	4	5
9.	I am tense and nervous while participating in group discussion.	1	2	3	4	5
10.	Although I talk fluently with friends, I am at a loss for words on the platform.	1	2	3	4	5
11.	I have no fear of expressing myself in a group.	1	2	3	4	5
12.	My hands tremble when I try to handle objects on the platform.	1	2	3	4	5
13.	I always avoid speaking in public if possible.	1	2	3	4	5
14.	I feel that I am more fluent when talking to people than most other people are.	1	2	3	4	5
15.	I am fearful and tense all the while I am speaking before a group of people.	1	2	3	4	5
16.	My thoughts become confused and jumbled when I speak before an audience.	1	2	3	4	5
17.	I like to get involved in group discussions.	1	2	3	4	5
18.	Although I am nervous just before getting up, I soon forget my fears and enjoy the experience.	1	2	3	4	5
19.	Conversing with people who hold positions of authority causes me to be fearful and tense.	1	2	3	4	5
20.	I dislike using my body and voice expressively.	1	2	3	4	5
21.	I feel relaxed and comfortable while speaking.	1	2	3	4	5
22.	I feel self-conscious when I am called upon to answer a question or give an opinion in class.	1	2	3	4	5
23.	I face the prospect of making a speech with complete confidence.	1	2	3	4	5
24.	I'm afraid to speak up in conversations.	1	2	3	4	5
25.	I would enjoy presenting a speech on a local television show.	1	2	3	4	5

FIGURE 7-1 (continued)

Scoring the PRCA

To compute your PRCA score, follow these 3 steps.
1. Add up your scores for items, 1, 3, 5, 8, 9, 10, 12, 13, 15, 16, 19, 20, 22, and 24.
2. Add up your scores for items 2, 4, 6, 7, 11, 14, 17, 18, 21, 23, and 25.
3. Complete the following formula:
    PRCA Score $= 84 -$ (total from step 1) $+$ (total from step 2)

(McCroskey, 1970)

FIGURE 7-2 Measure of Elementary Communication Apprehension

Directions for administering MECA: Tell the students that you will read each question and then they can find and circle the fact that shows how they feel. Put the following set of faces on the board. Explain the meaning of each face.

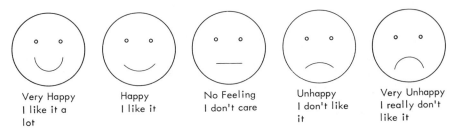

Very Happy	Happy	No Feeling	Unhappy	Very Unhappy
I like it a	I like it	I don't care	I don't like	I really don't
lot			it	like it

Complete some practice items with the students. When all questions have been answered, read each question to the students, allowing plenty of time for them to respond.

1. How do you feel about calling another student on the phone?
2. How do you feel when you know you have to give a report in class?
3. How do you feel about asking a clerk, or someone in a store, to help you?
4. How do you feel when your teacher calls on you to answer a question in class?
5. How do you feel about talking to adults?
6. How do you feel about talking a lot when you are on a bus?
7. How do you feel when you are picked to be a leader of a group?
8. How do you feel about talking a lot in class?
9. How do you feel about inviting your classmates to come to a party?
10. How do you feel about talking to other people?
11. How do you feel about trying to meet someone new?
12. How do you feel after you get up to talk in front of the class?
13. How do you feel when you know you have to give a speech?
14. How would you feel about giving a speech on television?
15. How do you feel about talking when you are in a small group?
16. How do you feel when you have to talk in a group?
17. How do you feel about talking to other students during recess?
18. How do you feel about talking to all of the people who sit close to you?
19. When someone comes to visit your class, how do you feel about asking them questions?
20. How do you feel when you talk in front of a large group of people?

(Garrison, J. P. & Garrison (Harris), K. R., 1977)

FIGURE 7-3 Writing Apprehension Test (WAT)

Directions: Below are a series of statements about writing. There are no right or wrong answers to these statements. Please indicate the degree to which each statement applies to you by marking whether you (1) Strongly Agree, (2) Agree, (3) Are Uncertain, (4) Disagree, or (5) Strongly Disagree with the statement. While some of these statements may seem repetitious, take your time and try to be as honest as possible.

	SA	A	UN	D	SD
1. I avoid writing.	1	2	3	4	5
2. I have no fear of my writing being evaluated.	1	2	3	4	5
3. I look forward to writing down my ideas.	1	2	3	4	5
4. My mind seems to go blank when I start to work on a composition.	1	2	3	4	5
5. Expressing ideas through writing seems to be a waste of time.	1	2	3	4	5
6. I would enjoy submitting my writing to magazines for evaluation and publication.	1	2	3	4	5
7. I like to write my ideas down.	1	2	3	4	5
8. I feel confident in my ability to clearly express my ideas in writing.	1	2	3	4	5
9. I like to have my friends read what I have written.	1	2	3	4	5
10. I'm nervous about writing.	1	2	3	4	5
11. People seem to enjoy what I write.	1	2	3	4	5
12. I enjoy writing.	1	2	3	4	5
13. I never seem to be able to clearly write down my ideas.	1	2	3	4	5
14. Writing is a lot of fun.	1	2	3	4	5
15. I like seeing my thoughts on paper.	1	2	3	4	5
16. Discussing my writing with others is an enjoyable experience.	1	2	3	4	5
17. It's easy for me to write good compositions.	1	2	3	4	5
18. I don't think I write as well as most other people.	1	2	3	4	5
19. I don't like my compositions to be evaluated.	1	2	3	4	5
20. I'm not good at writing.	1	2	3	4	5

Scoring the WAT

To compute your WAT score, follow these 3 steps.
1. Add up your scores for items 1, 4, 5, 10, 13, 18, 19, and 20.
2. Add up your scores for items 2, 3, 6, 7, 8, 9, 11, 12, 14, 15, 16, and 17.
3. Complete the following formula:
   WAT Score = 48 − (total from step 1) + (total from step 2)

(Daly & Miller, 1975)

Thus, examination of the theories of emotion provided a theoretical framework for the construct.

Theories of emotion can be divided into those which emphasize purely physiological processes, those which stress physiological factors and include awareness of psychological change, and those which attempt to interrelate physi-

FIGURE 7–4   Receiver Apprehension Test (RAT)

The following statements apply to how various people feel about receiving communication. Indicate if these statements apply to how you feel by noting whether you (1) Strongly Agree, (2) Agree, (3) Are Undecided, (4) Disagree, or (5) Strongly Disagree.

1. I feel comfortable when listening to others on the phone.
2. It is often difficult for me to concentrate on what others are saying.
3. When listening to members of the opposite sex I find it easy to concentrate on what is being said.
4. I have no fear of being a listener as a member of an audience.
5. I feel relaxed when listening to new ideas.
6. I would rather not have to listen to other people at all.
7. I am generally overexcited and rattled when others are speaking to me.
8. I often feel uncomfortable when listening to others.
9. My thoughts become confused and jumbled when reading important information.
10. I often have difficulty concentrating on what others are saying.
11. Receiving new information makes me feel restless.
12. Watching television makes me nervous.
13. When on a date I find myself tense and self-conscious when listening to my date.
14. I enjoy being a good listener.
15. I generally find it easy to concentrate on what is being said.
16. I seek out the opportunity to listen to new ideas.
17. I have difficulty concentrating on instructions others give me.
18. It is hard to listen or concentrate on what other people are saying unless I know them well.
19. I feel tense when listening as a member of a social gathering.
20. Television programs that attempt to change my mind about something make me nervous.

Wheeless (1975)

ological and cognitive factors. This third approach, advocated by Schachter (1964), synthesized the other two approaches and was formulated in response to severe criticisms of them. Schachter's theory, which suggests an interaction of cognitive and physiological determinants of emotional states, provides a useful theoretical framework for the explication of CA.

Schachter suggests that "an emotional state may be considered a function of a state of physiological arousal and of a cognition appropriate to this state of arousal" (1964, p. 51). This position implies that physiological arousal alone is not sufficient to induce an emotion, but some labeling of that emotion must also occur. Moreover, similar states of physiological arousal may be labeled differently depending on the cognitions arising from the immediate situation. This line of thought led Schachter to the following three predictions. First, given a state of physiological arousal for which an individual has no immediate explanation, he or she will label this state and describe feelings in terms of the cognitions available to him or her. Also, given a state of physiological arousal for which an individual has a completely appropriate explanation, no evaluative needs will arise and he or she will be unlikely to label feelings in terms of alter-nate cognitions available. Finally, in situations when cognitive circumstances are the same, the individual will describe feelings as emotions only to the extent that he or she experiences a state of physiological arousal (Schachter 1964, p. 53).

According to this theoretical perspective, a speaker will experience CA if he or she is physiologically aroused and can explain these feelings in terms of the speaking situation. Since past experience has indicated that fear of speaking before others is an appropriate explanation of his state of physiological arousal, it is unlikely that he would look elsewhere for alternative explanations. The theory would also predict that only those speakers who actually experience a state of physiological arousal would report an emotional reaction to the speaking situation. Most speakers probably do experience this state of physiological anxiety.

Although Schachter does not include a behavioral component in his theory, he clearly recognizes that an emotion may have behavioral manifestations. In fact, he has frequently used behavioral manifestations to infer emotional states. It seems logical then that research on CA would find interrelationships among the physiological, cognitive, and behavioral measures of CA. This was not the case, however, in the early research on CA. Clevenger's (1959) synthesis of this early research attempted to resolve the inconsistencies in the findings by positing three relatively independent dimensions of the construct:

> ... audience-perceived stage fright, cognitively-experienced stage fright, and physiological disruption are three variables which operate with only moderate interdependence during the course of a public speech. (Clevenger 1959, p. 138)

Although this hypothesis imposed some order on previously inconsistent research findings, it also identified a serious methodological problem that has continued to plague research in this area. If there are three independent dimensions of CA, then one alone cannot represent CA as a whole, nor can one dimension necessarily be expected to predict another. The implication is that it may be futile to attempt to validate a measurement of one dimension by correlating it with another. It remains unclear whether there are three relatively independent dimensions of the construct CA, or whether this independence is only an artifact of our measurement technique. In order to avoid this measurement dilemma, most researchers rely almost exclusively on the self-report method and specifically on the PRCA.

The second measurement problem concerns the classification of the PRCA scores into high, moderate, and low apprehensives. Usually this classification is made by using one standard deviation from the mean. For example, if the average score in your group was 75 and the standard deviation 10, then anyone scoring over 85 would be classified as a high CA individual and anyone scoring lower than 65 would be a low CA individual. Most researchers have used only high and low CA people as subjects and excluded the moderate CAs. The assumption has been that high CAs are the deviant individuals. Recent research, however, has begun to examine the moderate CA individuals and has discovered that they often are more similar to the high rather than the low CA individuals. Future researchers will probably focus more on the low CA people to see what makes them unique.

EFFECTS OF COMMUNICATION APPREHENSION ON CLASSROOM LEARNING

Classroom Behaviors

In the classroom, the high apprehensive student is at a disadvantage. He or she generally withdraws from the teacher and other students and may be labeled "shy."

On the basis of his observations of children in classes and college students in experimental situations, as well as of his shyness clinic, Zimbardo (1977) has drawn the following conclusions about shy students:

1. They are reluctant to initiate conversation, activities, add new ideas, volunteer, or ask questions.
2. They are reluctant to structure situations that are ambiguous.
3. As expected, shy students talk less than not-shys during most interactions with classmates. They allow more silent periods to develop and interrupt less than not-shys.
4. Unstructured permissive situations, such as a dance, create special problems for the shy that are not apparent when the guidelines for appropriate behavior are more spelled out, as in a lecture class.
5. In situations where initiative must be taken in male-female encounters, shy males have a harder time initiating conversations than shy females. (Men show decreased rates of talking and eye contact. Shy women react by smiling and nodding more when they are made more anxious.)
6. Shy students use fewer hand gestures during interviews than not-shy students.
7. Shy children spend more time in their seats, wander around less, and talk to fewer other children. They obey orders and are rarely troublesome.
8. Rarely are the shy chosen for special duties such as teacher's errand monitor.
9. They get fewer social rewards and give fewer strokes in return than do the not-shys. (pp. 68–69)

These shy students will probably choose classroom seats in the back and sides of the room, areas away from high interaction zones. Rarely will these students volunteer to participate in classroom oral activities. If they are forced to participate in a group discussion, the few comments they contribute may be irrelevant to the group's interaction. These highly apprehensive students will not assume leadership positions. In fact, their style of communication probably will suggest a lack of self-confidence. Powers (1977) found that these apprehensive students used more rhetorical interrogatives in their communication. Moreover, fewer original ideas will be contributed by these students.

Overall Educational Achievement

This reluctance to communicate generally leads to poor educational achievement. High apprehensive students usually have lower college grade point averages and lower overall academic achievement than low apprehensives. They prefer large lecture classes and are not at a disadvantage in them.

However, in smaller classes where more oral communication is required the high apprehensive students perform more poorly than the low apprehensives (McCroskey & Andersen 1976). If these students are experiencing difficulty in a class, they are unlikely to seek the assistance of available tutors (Scott, Yates, & Wheeless 1975). For example, consider the case of John R., a high communication apprehensive high school student.

When John R.'s name comes up in the teacher's lounge, it will probably be associated with such descriptions as curt, tight-lipped, uncommunicative, shifty, shy, withdrawn, close mouthed, fearful, apprehensive, or antisocial.

John can be observed as always on the fringes of social gatherings. He usually eats alone in the cafeteria and walks to classes by himself. He sits in the back of the room and if called upon will feel shakiness, butterflies, rapid heartbeat, and nausea. If he responds to the question with anything other than a mumbled "I don't know," his answer will probably terminate abruptly. If the teacher challenges his answer, he's apt to become unnaturally apologetic.

Even when John has finished, he is still likely to feel all the previous unpleasant sensations. He would much rather write a paper than give an oral report, and he expresses himself well in writing.

If John has to become part of a group project, he will tend to say very little, seem uninterested in the group's activities, and will occasionally make an unrelated contribution.

Even though John is not doing well in class, he seldom seeks help from his teacher. His parents might be unaware of his problem at school because he rarely talks things over with his parents.

John feels awkward in any social situation. He is attracted to a girl in the class, Sue, and even though he thinks she has smiled at him before, he is fairly certain that the smile was intended for someone else. Anyway, he decides to wait until she starts a conversation with him. Above all, he wishes he had the poise and self-confidence that he believes all the other kids have.

If you asked other students about John, they would probably say that they are not very attracted to him and certainly wouldn't want him to be a leader in their social group. They would probably see him as a trustworthy but not an authoritative or dynamic speaker.

John's future may not be too bright. He is less likely to start college than many of his less apprehensive peers. If required to take a public speaking course, he may drop out of college. He will probably choose to live in an isolated apartment or dormitory room and to select as many mass lecture courses as possible. Later when John seeks a job, he will likely be seen as a weaker job candidate unless the job requires little communication.

Reasons for Poor Performance

Clearly, the highly apprehensive student performs more poorly in school. But why? Perhaps those students with high apprehension have less ability. This explanation has not been supported by the research, however. No relationship has been found between communication apprehension and intelligence (McCroskey, Daly, & Sorensen 1976). Moreover, high communication apprehensives do achieve at comparable levels with other students in some instructional environments, for example, the large lecture class.

Teachers' expectancies is another potential explanation of the poorer academic achievement of high communication apprehensive students. Since the publication of *Pygmalion in the Classroom* (Rosenthal & Jacobson 1968), there has been increased interest in the effects of teachers' expectations on the achievement of their students. McCroskey and Daly (1976) investigated teachers' expectancies of high and low apprehensive elementary school children. They constructed the following two descriptions of hypothetical elementary school children.

> Jimmy T. was born in this community and has lived here all his life. His parents own and operate a local business. Jimmy is a very quiet child who seldom volunteers to participate in class. In fact, some days I hardly know he is in class, since he sits in the back of the room. However, his attendance is very good except when he is scheduled to make a presentation before the class. He seems to prefer to work alone rather than with a group. His written work is almost always turned in on time. I have found it hard to get to know Jimmy because he is so reticent with me. His previous teachers have also commented about what a nice, quiet boy Jimmy is.
>
> Billy G. was born in this community and has lived here all his life. His parents own and operate a local business. You always know that Billy is present, because he sits right in front of the room. His attendance is very good. Billy seems to enjoy making presentations to the class and working on group projects. His written work is almost always turned in on time. I have found it very easy to get to know Billy because he likes to talk with me. His previous teachers have also commented about what a nice, outgoing boy Billy is. (McCroskey & Daly, 1976, pp. 68–69.)

Elementary school teachers were given one of these descriptions and asked to estimate the child's success in the following nine areas: reading, arithmetic, social studies, science, art, deportment, class participation, relationships with other students, and overall achievement. The results show that the low apprehensive child (Billy) would do better in all academic areas than the high apprehensive child (Jimmy). In addition, Billy was expected to have much greater likelihood of positive relationships with other students than Jimmy. Clearly, the teachers studied had much higher expectations for the low apprehensive students. Such expectations may become self-fulfilling prophecies. Teachers may have a bias against quiet children, or they may be responding to what they have seen happen to quiet children in the classroom.

A third possible reason for the high communication apprehensive students' poorer academic performance may be the attitudes of the students themselves. In a study of junior high school boys (Hurt, Preiss, & Davis 1976), high communication apprehensive boys had a more negative attitude toward school than low apprehensive boys. Similar results were found in a study of college students (McCroskey & Andersen 1976). Its unclear, however, whether high apprehension causes negative attitudes which result in lower achievement, or high apprehension causes lower achievement which results in negative attitudes toward school.

Lack of self-esteem is related to high CA although its not possible to determine if its a cause or an effect. An individual's image of self is related to many indexes of social adjustment. McCroskey and others (1977) studied the direct relationship between self-esteem and oral communication apprehension. Results from two college student samples, two samples of elementary and secondary teachers, and a sample of federal employees indicate highly consistent correlations across age groups and occupational types. Zimbardo (1700) reports a similar relationship between self-esteem and shyness for young children. In his interviews with children, Zimbardo found that boys feel they are too tall, too fat, too weak, too ugly, less strong, and generally less attractive than their not-shy classmates. The shy girls are more likely to describe themselves as thin, unattractive, and less intelligent than their peers. None of these children feels he or she is "popular," and three-fourths say they are downright "unpopular." However, ironically, not-shy children say they like being alone more than shy students.

How do these individuals develop such negative self-images? Generally, we know that people derive their feelings about self from interactions with others. The apprehensive person derives few positive appraisals from his relationships. McCroskey (1977) summarized other people's perceptions of the high CA individual with the proposition that people who experience a high level of CA will be perceived less positively by others in their environment than will people who experience lower levels of CA. Zimbardo (1977) provides a dramatic example of these negative perceptions:

> I was a very sensitive, highly nervous, self-conscious child, so much so that my parents, with a well-meant but mistaken idea, decided to keep me home to protect me. I was denied formal education, only one room coun-

try school part time until I was sixteen. I knew I was different from my sisters and brothers and tried to hide it, which didn't help. When I was five an aunt (who painted beautifully without any lessons) stood behind me one day and said, "Huh! She's going to be an artist and they are all queer." I never forgot that. (p. 58)

Knutson and Lashbrook's (1976) research on CA and social style found that people with high CA were perceived as low in both assertiveness and responsiveness. Merrill's (1974) earlier research characterized unresponsive persons as cool, independent, uncommunicative, disciplined, rational, hard-to-know, task oriented, and businesslike. People perceived as low in assertiveness were characterized as cooperative, risk avoiding, slow to take action, "go-along" persons, and nondirective.

Freimuth (1976) examined the interpersonal implications of CA by looking at the effects of a sender's CA on receivers. The results showed that senders' CA had a negative effect on receivers comprehension and ratings of authoritativeness. This relationship did not hold for receivers' ratings on character. The strongest relationship between the set of CA variables and the set of communication effectiveness variables indicated that individuals who reported high apprehension experienced much silence in their speech and received low ratings particularly on language facility, vocal characteristics, and general effectiveness. Each of these studies shows that the behaviors characteristic of the communication of high CA individuals are associated with negative perceptions from other people.

McCroskey (1977) summarizes a group of studies to further support this contention. These studies show that people with high CA are perceived as less socially attractive, less task attractive, less competent, less sexually attractive, less attractive as a communication partner, less sociable, less composed, and less extroverted, but of slightly higher character.

The following story of Jay Jay, cited by Zimbardo (1977) and related by Marilynne Robinson, a second grade teacher, illustrates the way schools can create and reinforce these negative self-images.

Jay Jay was a loving eager child, entering second grade. He came from a low socioeconomic background and spoke pidgin English in first grade. Our school at that time sent all their children out to top, middle, and low reading groups, much to my dismay. I was ineffectual in getting the "higher ups" to change this, so I offered to take the "low group." I had great visions of improving self-images, and starting these children on the road to becoming great readers. The children soon got the picture that they were in the low group and that there was no way to move up. The middle and high classes were too full.

Jay Jay was teased about being in the low group, but continued to work hard. As the years went by, Jay continued to be in the low groups. There's rarely a way to move up, once one is labeled in the early years.

Jay Jay found he had some esteem by being an excellent athlete. This worked well for him until his friends grew in size, and he remained small.

At the intermediate school there were no longer any recesses to play ball. Now it was real competition in sports. The big boys made the team. The small boys, like shy Jay Jay, didn't qualify for the "real" sports.

Jay Jay is now entering the eighth grade. If he can excel at the high-jacking game ("You got quartah?—Search—Take"), or gambling in the bathrooms, he may make it in the underworld, and perhaps end up in another one of society's institutions—prison. (pp. 67–68)

CAUSES OF COMMUNICATION APPREHENSION

Since high communication apprehension is so detrimental to learning, prevention of its development is the best strategy for educators. First, the causes of communication apprehension must be determined. The existing research is limited. Daly and Friedrich (1978) have outlined four potential causes: genetic predisposition, reinforcement, skills acquisition, and modeling.

Genetic Predisposition

The genetic predisposition explanation suggests that there is some genetic component to communication apprehension. Although no research yet has directly examined this explanation of the development of communication apprehension, research comparing the sociability of identical and fraternal twins does offer some support for this theory. Even if there is some genetic predisposition for communication apprehension, the environment will certainly enhance or minimize its development.

Reinforcement

Reinforcement is probably the most popular explanation for the development of communication apprehension. Basically reinforcement theory suggests that a child learns to repeat behaviors that are rewarded, while behaviors that are not rewarded are eliminated over time. A child who is rewarded for being silent and who is not rewarded (or perhaps even punished) for talking will become a quiet child. Moreover, this quiet child will have fewer opportunities to acquire skills necessary to communicate successfully and consequently will experience few rewards when he or she does try to talk.

While the reinforcement theory seems to be reasonable explanation for the development of communication apprehension, it does not explain why some children are given this kind of reinforcement. The few tentative reasons offered focus on the child's family. For example, Phillips and Butt (1966) found that a disproportionately large percentage of high communication apprehensive college students reported being from first and second generation ethnic families. Perhaps these children have difficulty acquiring language skills or have parents who are poor communication models.

Parents' attitudes toward communication is another explanation for the development of CA advanced by Phillips (1968). He suggests that if parents use communication as a weapon, children may be conditioned to avoid communication to escape such abuse. These children may fail to learn that communicating can also offer positive rewards.

Zimbardo (1977) cites an example of such a case.

> My shyness was prompted by my ungrateful sober father whose disposition can be likened only to Sir Walter Scotts' description of his father: "A man with a temper constantly unstrung who disapproved of anything and everything we tried to do to please him; who spoke with a forcefulness that no one dared or could ignore." So, shy I was for many years out of sheer frustration. (p. 58)

A rural environment may be a factor in the development of high levels of CA suggests the results of two studies (Grutzeck 1970; Richmond & Robertson 1977). Children growing up in rural areas may be exposed to fewer adults and fewer situations demanding effective communication. Thus, these rural children may develop fewer communication skills and therefore receive less reinforcement for communicating.

Skill Acquisition

The skill acquisition theory suggests that a child becomes apprehensive because of a failure to develop the skills necessary for successful communication. This explanation is closely related to the reinforcement explanation.

Modeling

The modeling theory explains high CA as developing from imitation of others whom the child observes in social interaction. This explanation would suggest that high apprehensive parents would have high apprehensive children.

Zimbardo (1977) and his associates observed every grade from nursery school through junior high in several Palo Alto, California schools and interviewed and surveyed the parents of the children in those schools. They found that about 70 percent of the time parents and children tend to be shy together. However the relationship between parent and child shyness is not that simple. While shy children are not likely in families where both parents are not shy, having at least one shy parent increases the chances a child will become shy. Yet, families with two shy parents don't have any more shy children than those with only one shy parent. Moreover, the brothers and sisters of the shy child tended to be not shy. Zimbardo suggests that shy parents are likely to have one child who is shy, and that child is probably their first.

TREATMENT OF COMMUNICATION APPREHENSION

Prevention

There are several methods available to treat high levels of CA. Prevention, however, is obviously better than treatment. McCroskey (1977) recommends the following steps to reduce the chance of a child developing high CA:

1. Extra effort should be exerted to provide children with reinforcement for their communication during their formative years, particularly in large families.
2. Children with slow language development or deficient speech skills should receive help as early as possible so that they do not lose positive reinforcement as a result of deficient skills.
3. Teachers should be trained to recognize the presence of CA in a child and provide extra reinforcement for the child's communication, particularly in the early school years.
4. Classroom teaching procedures should be modified so that children are not required to perform orally at a level beyond their skill development, such as eliminating required oral reading of material in the first and second grades that includes sounds that the child has not yet mastered. (p. 92)

Zimbardo (1977) quotes Marilynne Robinson, a gifted second grade teacher discussing the problem of shyness as follows:

> Children who are shy in the classroom fear running and dancing to rhythm records. Their voices can barely be heard asking a question, and will frequently answer, "I don't know." They are afraid to sing out, speak out, and in general, afraid to make mistakes. They sit back and wait for someone to ask them to play. If this doesn't happen they may wander around the playground sometimes finding a "sore finger" so that they may see the nurse.
> As long as parents, the community, and the institutions place such strong emphasis on grades and reading level, our children will feel less confident and less able to feel joy in their lives. Due to the strong emphasis on being able to read in our institutions, those with a slower start are disadvantaged to begin with. They become real prisoners in our schools. (p. 66)

Communication teachers need to be especially sensitive to communication apprehension. Since many communication courses require some performance, highly apprehensive students may have serious difficulty in these courses. The old adage "Get them up to speak—experience reduces nervousness" may work for the average student but can be disastrous for the student with high CA. McCroskey (1977a) reports that high apprehensives drop public speaking courses in disproportionately high percentages (50 to 70 percent) even when the course is required. While communication courses generally reduce anxiety for most students, some students may experience negative effects. For example, Brooks and Platz (1968) found that one-fourth of students in speech classes had lower self-concepts after the course even though three-fourths improved their communication self-concept.

McCroskey (1977b) offers some general advice to classroom teachers to help the apprehensive student be successful. Most importantly, he warns against forcing an apprehensive child to communicate. A teacher can provide assignments as alternatives to oral performance activities and can strive to create an instructional environment which does not punish the quieter students. Allowing students to select their own seats is recommended because students will choose places which are comfortable for them.

According to research by Burgoon (1975), anxious students prefer activities which minimize the need for communication. They prefer written to oral assignments, lectures over class discussions, written tests rather than oral evaluations, grades based on test performance rather than class participation, and grades based on the quality of written work rather than the quality of oral presentations. If a communication course is performance oriented and elective, its unlikely that any high apprehensives will enroll and hence no problem exists for the instructor. If a communication course is required, students might be given an option of a performance or nonperformance based course. If this option is not feasible, then a program to reduce communication apprehension should be available for the high apprehensives.

Programs to Reduce Communication Apprehension

The treatment most widely used is systematic desensitization (SD). SD has become a popular method of treatment because it is highly effective, easy to administer, and relatively inexpensive. SD usually involves learning a complete muscular relaxation procedure. The individual then constructs a hierarchy of fearful speaking situations which might range from talking to your best friend to giving a speech on national television. After the hierarchy is developed, the individual, in a state of relaxation, is told to imagine the least threatening situation and to continue relaxing. The individual works up the hierarchy until able to relax while imagining the top hierarchy situation. The theory behind SD is that one eliminates the anxiety response through a counterconditioning process that pairs the threatening stimulus with a relaxation response rather than with heightened arousal. Variations in the traditional SD procedures such as administration to groups rather than individuals and audiotaped self-administered SD seem to be equally effective.

Rational Emotive Therapy (RET) stresses cognitive processes, emphasizes the need to alter the individual's thinking in order to reduce symptoms, and suggests how thinking should be modified. RET was developed by Ellis (1958) and is based on the idea that people become anxious because of irrational thinking.

If the irrational thinking can be deconditioned, then the anxiety will be eliminated. For example, a man is about to be interviewed for a job and says to himself "It will be awful if the managar thinks I'm dumb and can't do the job." A strong anxiety response follows. According to RET, the anxiety response would not have occurred if the man had told himself (rationally) "It's impossible to impress everyone. I'll do my best and if he doesn't hire me, there are always other jobs." The objective of RET is to teach people to substitute rational for irrational self-verbalizations. It must be remembered that RET is a therapeutic technique that should only be used by persons who have been trained by a professional clinician.

Phillips and Metzger (1973) advocated treating reticence through Reality Therapy, a treatment developed by Glaser in 1965. This therapy centers on learning to change communication behavior in a wide range of situations, but also permits consideration of associated changes in perceptions and emotions.

Reality Therapy breaks down into three steps, the first of which is goal setting. These goals must be accomplishable, involving specific behavior or achievement as an end product. Steps in progression to help achieve each goal must be listed along with guidelines for judging progress toward the goal. Alternative ways to achieve the goal must also be developed. The second step is to list these goals in order of difficulty so that the subject can work on the easiest goal first and then move on to the more difficult goals. The third step is to group subjects according to goals. This group with similar goals, along with the instructor, can then plan a program to afford goal achievement.

More recently Phillips (1977) described his treatment approach as rejecting the physiological model of CA and advocating a rhetorical view of speech problems which attempts to discover who needs what kind of instruction. Anxiety is not mentioned unless the reticent person brings it up. Instead the rhetoritherapist tries to discover how well the reticent person manages the subprocesses in the rhetorical use of speech by asking the following questions:

1. Can the client perceive situations in which his talk would make a difference?
2. Can he identify relevant people in his environment, the modification of whose ideas or actions may be valuable to him?
3. Can he specify communication goals?
4. Does he have a flexible repertoire of roles available so he can adapt himself to intellectual, emotional, and situational needs of his listeners?
5. Can he conceptualize ideas to be spoken?
6. Does he have sufficient command of language to handle his needs?
7. Can he perform basic speech acts?
8. Does he assess responses accurately? (p. 43)

A negative answer to any of these questions defines an instructional goal for rhetoritherapy.

SUMMARY

Anxiety about oral communication has been given many labels. Stage fright refers to fear of public speaking and is the same as state communication apprehension. Trait communication apprehension, also called reticence and shyness, is a broad-based fear of communicating. Individuals with high levels of CA are people for whom the apprehension about participating in communication outweighs the projected gain. These individuals will generally avoid communication if possible or suffer from a variety of anxiety-type feelings when forced to communicate.

Almost everyone occasionally experiences state CA and it is considered a normal reaction to a performance situation. Trait CA, however, is an abnormal reaction to oral communication experienced by 15 to 20 percent of American college students.

Two other forms of communication apprehension with serious consequences for the classroom have been identified—writing apprehension and receiver apprehension. Students with writing apprehension are the individuals who consistently fail to turn in writing assignments, who do not attend class when writing is required, and who seldom voluntarily enroll in courses which demand writing. Receiver apprehension may affect one's ability to process information and to adjust psychologically to messages sent by others.

Although CA may be measured physiologically, behaviorally, and psychologically, the most useful approach for the classroom teacher is the psychological or self-report measure. The *Personal Report of Communication Apprehension* (PRCA) is the scale most commonly used. A scale similar to the PRCA has been developed for preliterate children, the *Measure of Elementary Communication Apprehension* (MECA). A similar self-report measure can be used to assess writing apprehension, the *Writing Apprehension Test* (WAT).

The student with high CA is at a disadvantage in the classroom. He or she may be labeled shy and will not participate in most discussions. These highly apprehensive students will probably have lower grade point averages and overall academic achievement. This lower achievement cannot be attributed to lower ability since no relationship has been found between apprehension and intelligence. Three other reasons for the lower achievement have been suggested. Teachers may have lowered expectations for the quiet children and these expectations may be self-fulfilling. On the other hand, high CA students may have negative attitudes toward school, which results in lowered achievement. Although its not possible to determine the cause-effect nature of the relationship, high CA individuals tend to have lower self-esteem than low CA people.

Obviously it is important to attempt to prevent the development of CA in children. The first step in prevention is the identification of the causes of CA. Four potential causes have been suggested: genetic predisposition, reinforcement, skills acquisition, and modeling. Reinforcement is probably the most popular explanation for the development of CA. Basically, reinforcement theory suggests that a child who is rewarded for being silent and who is not rewarded (or even punished) for talking becomes a quiet child. Family characteristics are being investigated as potential reasons for these reinforcement patterns.

Prevention is better than treatment. The chapter suggests several steps which parents and teachers can take to prevent the development of CA in children. Communication teachers have a special responsibility to deal with the problem of CA in their classrooms. Several suggestions are given.

Three programs to reduce CA are systematic desensitization (SD), Rational-emotive therapy (RET), and rhetoritherapy. SD is the most popular method of treatment because it is highly effective, easy to administer, and relatively inexpensive. The most common form of this treatment involves complete muscular relaxation and a pairing of that relaxed state to a hierarchy of communication situations. RET is a method of restructuring cognitive processes. The objective is to teach people to substitute rational for irrational self-verbalizations. Rhetoritherapy advocates a rhetorical view of speech problems and attempts to discover who needs what kind of instruction.

SUGGESTED READINGS

DALY, J. A. and M. D. MILLER. "The empirical development of an instrument to measure writing apprehension." *Research in the Teaching of English,* 1975, *9,* 242–49.

> The original report of the *Writing Apprehension Test* with a rationale for the importance of studying this form of communication apprehension. A copy of the WAT is included as well as a discussion of its reliability and validity.

McCROSKEY, J. C. "The implementation of a large-scale program of systematic desensitization for communication apprehension." *The Speech Teacher,* 1972, *21,* 255–64.

> A report of an extensive treatment program for communication apprehension and discussion of how a similar program can be implemented in other places. The article discusses the muscular relaxation procedure and the hierarchy of fearful speaking situations.

McCROSKEY, J. C. "Classroom consequences of communication apprehension." *Communication Education,* 1977, *26,* 27–33.

> A review of the effects of communication apprehension in the classroom. The article discusses the causes of the classroom effects and the implications for classroom teachers.

McCROSKEY, J. C. "Oral Communication apprehension: A summary of recent theory and research." *Human Communication Research,* 1977, *4,* 78–96.

> A state of the art review of research in communication apprehension. The article examines the nature of CA, the causes, its measurement, correlates, effects, treatment, prevention, and future research.

McCROSKEY, J. C.   *Quiet Children and the Classroom Teacher.* Urbana, Ill.: ERIC clearinghouse on reading and communication skills (SCA publication), 1977.

A good summary of research on communication apprehension for the classroom teacher who has not read much of the published literature on communication apprehension. The booklet includes scales for diagnosing CA.

PHILLIPS, G. M.   "Reticence: Pathology of the normal speaker." *Speech Monographs,* 1968, *35,* 38–49.

A theoretical discussion of the causes and effects of oral communication apprehension.

ZIMBARDO, P. G.   *Shyness.* Reading, Mass.: Addison-Wesley Publishing Co., Inc., 1977.

An interesting discussion of shyness—what it is and what one can do about it. The book is a compilation of personal observations and empirical research on shyness as well as practical suggestions for overcoming the problem.

REFERENCES

BROOKS, W. D., and S. M. PLATZ. "The effects of speech training upon self concept as a communicator." *The Speech Teacher,* 1968, *17,* 44–49.

BRUSKIN ASSOCIATES. "What are Americans afraid of?" *The Bruskin Report,* 1973, no. 53.

BURGOON, J. K. "Teacher strategies for coping with communication apprehension." Paper presented to the Speech Communication Association, Houston, Texas, 1975.

BURGOON, J. K. "The unwillingness to communicate scale: Development and validation." *Communication Monographs,* 1976, *43,* 60–69.

CLEVENGER, T., Jr. "A definition of stage fright." *Central States Speech Journal,* 1955, *7,* 26–30.

CLEVENGER, T., Jr. "A synthesis of experimental research in stage fright." *Quarterly Journal of Speech,* 1959, *45,* 134–45.

CLEVENGER, T., Jr., and T. R. KING. "A factor analysis of the visible symptoms of stage fright." *Speech Monographs,* 1961, *28,* 296–98.

DALY, J. A. and G. FRIEDRICH. "The Development of Communication Apprehension; A Retrospective Analysis of Some Contributory Correlates," A paper prepared for the Annual Convention of the Speech Communication Association. Minneapolis, Nov. 2–5, 1968.

DALY, J. A., and M. D. MILLER. "The empirical development of an instrument to measure writing apprehension." *Research in the Teaching of English,* 1975, *9,* 242–49.

ELLIS, A. "Rational psychotherapy." *Journal of General Psychology,* 1958, *59,* 35–49.

FREIMUTH, V. S. "Apprehension and communication effectiveness." *Human Communication Research,* 1976, *2* (3), 289–98.

GARRISON, K. R., and J. P. GARRISON. "Measurement of Communication Apprehension Among Children," Paper presented to the International Communication Association Convention, Berlin, 1977.

GARRISON, J. P., and K. R. GARRISON. "Measurement of oral communication apprehension among children: A factor in the development of basic speech skills." *Communication Education*, 1979, *28*, 119-28.

GRUTZEK, L. F. "A search for invariant characteristics of reticent elementary school children." M. A. Thesis, Pennsylvania State University, 1970.

HURT, H. T., R. PREISS, and B. DAVIS. "The effects of communication apprehension of middle-school children on sociometric choice, affective and cognitive learning." Paper presented at the International Communication Association Convention, Portland, Oregon, 1976.

KNUTSON, P. K., and W. B. LASHBROOK. "Communication apprehension as an antecedent to social style." Paper presented to the Speech Communication Association Convention, San Francisco, 1976.

LAMB, D. H. "Speech anxiety: Towards a theoretical conceptualization and preliminary scale development." *Speech Monographs*, 1972, *39*, 62-67.

McCROSKEY, J. C. "Measures of Communication—Bound Anxiety." *Speech Monographs*, 1970, (37), p. 269-77.

McCROSKEY, J. C. "Validity of the PRCA as an index of oral communication apprehension." Paper presented to the Speech Communication Association Convention, Houston, Texas, 1975.

McCROSKEY, J. C. "Oral communication apprehension: A summary of recent theory and research." *Human Communication Research*, 1977a, *4*, 78-96.

McCROSKEY, J. C. *Quiet Children and the Classroom Teacher*. Urbana, Ill.: ERIC Clearinghouse on reading and communication skills (SCA publication) 1977b.

McCROSKEY, J. C. "Classroom consequences of communication apprehension." *Communication Education*, 1977c, *26*, 27-33.

McCROSKEY, J. C., and J. F. ANDERSON. "Teachers' expectations of the communication apprehensive child in the elementary school." *Human Communication Research*, 1976, *3*, 67-72.

McCROSKEY, J. C., J. A. DALY, and G. A. SORENSEN. "Personality correlates of communication apprehension." *Human Communication Research*, 1976, *2*, 376-81.

McCROSKEY, J. C. and J. A. DALY. "Teacher's Expectations of the Communication Apprehensive Child in the Elementary School." *Human Communication Research*, 1976 (3), p. 67-72.

McCROSKEY, J. C., J. A. DALY, V. P. RICHMOND, and R. L. FALCIONE. "Studies of the relationship between communication apprehension and self-esteem." *Human Communication Research*, 1977, *3*, 269-77.

MERRILL, D. *Reference Survey Profile*. Denver: Personal Predictions and Research, Inc., 1974.

MULAC, A., and A. R. SHERMAN. "Behavioral assessment of speech anxiety." *Quarterly Journal of Speech*, 1974, *60*, 134-43.

PHILLIPS, G. M. "Reticence: Pathology of the normal speaker." *Speech Monographs*, 1968, *35*, 39-49.

PHILLIPS, G. M. "Rhetoritherapy versus the medical model: Dealing with reticence." *Communication Education*, 1977, *26*, 34-43.

PHILLIPS, G. M., and D. BUTT. "Reticence revisited." *Pennsylvania Speech Annual*, 1966, *23*, 40-57.

PHILLIPS, G. M., and N. J. METZGER. "The Reticent Syndrome: Some theoretical considerations about etiology and treatment." *Speech Monographs.* 1973, *40,* 220–30.

PORTER, D. T. "Communication apprehension: Communication's latest artifact?" Paper presented at the annual meeting of the International Communication Association, Philadelphia, May 1979.

POWERS, W. G. "The rhetorical interrogative: Anxiety or control?" *Human Communication Research,* 1977, *4,* 44–47.

RADL, S. "Why you are shy and how to cope with it." *Glamour,* June 1976, 64, 84.

RICHMOND, V. P. and D. ROBERTSON. "Communication apprehension as a function of being raised in an urban or rural environment." Unpublished monograph, West Virginia Northern Community College, 1977.

ROSENTHAL, R. and L. JACOBSON. *Pygmalion in the Classroom: Teacher Expectation and Pupils' Intellectual Development.* New York: Holt, Rinehart & Winston, 1968.

SCHACHTER, S. "The interaction of cognitive and physiological determinants of emotional state." In Berkowitz (ed.), *Advances in Experimental Social Psychology.* New York: Academic Press, Inc., 1964.

SCOTT, M. D., M. P. YATES, and L. R. WHEELESS. "An exploratory investigation of the effects of communication apprehension in alternative systems of instruction." Paper presented to International Communication Association Convention, Chicago, 1975.

SPIELBERGER, C. D. (ed.) *Anxiety and Behavior.* New York: Academic Press, Inc., 1966.

WHEELESS, L. R. "An investigation of receiver apprehension and social context dimensions of communication apprehension." *The Speech Teacher,* 1975, *24* (3), 261–68.

ZIMBARDO, P. G. *Shyness.* Reading, Mass.: Addison-Wesley Publishing Co., Inc., 1977.

CHAPTER EIGHT
SELF-CONCEPT, SIGNIFICANT OTHERS, AND CLASSROOM COMMUNICATION

Jean M. Civikly*

*Dr. Civikly is Associate Professor, Department of Speech Communication, at the University of New Mexico.

In a recent review of research on self-concept, Morris Rosenberg (1979) observed that "it is somewhat astonishing to think that after decades of theory and research on the self-concept, investigators are as far as ever from agreeing on what it is or what it includes. . . . In fact, . . . the 'self' stands as a concept foremost in the ranks of confusion."

The intent of this chapter is to dissipate some of this "confusion" and clarify selected issues of self-concept as they relate to theory and research on effective classroom communication and instruction. Two questions underscore the writing and reading of this chapter: (1) Why should teachers be concerned with information about self-concept? and (2) How might teachers use this information to enhance student self-concept and academic performance?

CONCEPTUAL FRAMEWORK

Defining Terms

Following the advice of the King of Hearts to the White Rabbit to "begin at the beginning," a distinction of the terms *self-concept* and *self-esteem* is in order. *Self-concept* is defined as the totality of *descriptions* which a person holds for self. These descriptions of self are hinted at when a person responds to questions such as Who are you? How would you describe yourself?, and include such features as the person's ideas about self, and his or her most characteristic traits, actions, beliefs. *Self-esteem* is defined as the totality of *evaluations* which a person holds about self. These judgments of self can be gleaned from responses to questions such as What do you like about yourself? and What don't you like about yourself? Two people may have similar self-concepts, which might include the rather stable features "honest, modest, stubborn, artistic, compulsive, . . ." For one person self-esteem may be moderate, since the person likes being honest and artistic but may dislike the stubborn-modest-compulsive side. For the other person self-esteem may be high, since the individual views each trait positively. As can be seen, self-esteem is a calculation, a decision, an evaluation of a set of behavioral and attitudinal characteristics, and it varies with the individual. While self-concept is more stable and enduring, self-esteem may vary by the day or hour.

Dimensions of Self-Concept

When viewing teachers and students in the wide variety of instructional arenas, analysis of the breadth of self-concept is crucial. As viewed by Rosenberg (1979), the self-concept can be categorized in three ways: (1) how you view yourself (the extant self), (2) how you would like to see yourself (the desired self), and (3) how you show yourself to others (the presenting self).

The *extant self,* how you see yourself, is quite elaborate. It includes your view of your *social status,* as measured by your perception of such factors as your sex, age, family reputation, socioeconomic status, and occupational position; your identity with *membership groups* related to religion, ethnicity and politics; *social labels* assigned to you by yourself or others (for example, intellectual, alcoholic, athletic); *past group identities* (for example, divorcée, reformed addict, Harvard graduate); and *"ego-extensions,"* the material objects you possess or by which you are identified—your clothes, property, and personal possessions. Using these factors as a basis for self-description, imagine the variety of "selves" rampant in a class of even ten or twenty people. Now, add to these descriptions the way each individual would *like* to see him- or herself, that is, the desired self-concepts, and the classroom dynamics become even more complex.

As is true with the extant self, there is a range of possible manifestations of the *desired self.* There is the *idealized* image, one which is very nice to contemplate but is more fantasy than realism—you want to be perfectly perfect. There is also the *committed* image and the *moral* image. The committed image is the one which an individual makes efforts to actually attain. It includes desirable behaviors which appear to the individual to be within the realm of the possible, the achievable—for example, finishing college, going to graduate school. The *moral* image is what the individual thinks he or she should be—those messages of conscience which twirl one's mind—"Don't be selfish. Share what you have." While each of these images of the desired self-concept plays a role in how individuals present themselves to others, for the teacher it would be most productive to discover each student's committed self, since this is the force which the *student* sees as motivating. It is expected that accomplishments in the area of the student's committed self, those areas which the student views as meriting his or her concerted efforts, will be more rapid as they have that key distinction of student self-motivation. The student's committed self-image, if not directly in line with the teacher's preferences, can still serve as a starting point for achievements on which the student and teacher may reach some future compromise.

The third aspect of the self-concept, the *presenting self,* involves the ways in which an individual behaves and how the individual shows himself or herself to others. As noted by Rosenberg (1979), the presenting self is of importance throughout the life cycle but is tested most repeatedly during the adolescent years.

> For youth, in particular, self-presentation is likely to assume the function of testing, and attempting to validate, one or more self-hypotheses. The adolescent may thus reflect on many different possible selves, playing diverse roles, cultivating diverse abilities, and experimenting with different traits. In a groping and tentative way, different selves may be rehearsed—the glamor girl, the caustic wit, the world-weary sophisticate, the dedicated revolutionary. Selves may be tried on or discarded like garments as ado-

lescents attempt to convince others of their sophistication, their cheerful-
ness, their allure, their intelligence. Hence the common sense question:
"What is he (she) trying to prove?" has profound psychological significance, for this is precisely what the adolescent is trying to do. A girl wants
a date in order to have *evidence* that she is attractive or lovable. A boy
wants to succeed in school in order to gain *evidence* that he is intelligent.
What concerns these youngsters is the *uncertainty* about what they are
like; what motivates them is the desire to know, to achieve certainty.
When an adolescent—or anyone else—tries to achieve a certain goal, he does
so not simply for the direct advantage it affords, but because it enables
him to prove something about himself to himself. Yet ultimate certainty
forever eludes us so that the responses of others are required not only
for confirmation but for the lifelong reconfirmation of our working self-
hypotheses. (pp. 48–49)

Of course, it would be a simpler world, although assuredly less fascinating,
if the self one presented and saw in social situations reflected precisely the view
held by each person. But we are not always so translucent; and at times, social
interactions may dictate that the presenting self not reflect the extant and desired
self so that social tact and acceptance will be maintained. Thus, the presenting
self of the teacher and students may not necessarily be in agreement with the extant and desired selves. Also, based on these three aspects of self-concept (the
extant, desired, and presenting selves), it would seem instrumental for a teacher,
at any level of the educational process, to identify in self and students each of
these aspects and their subcomponents and to use this information in the development and adjustment of instructional content and strategies.

THEORIES OF SELF-CONCEPT DEVELOPMENT AND ENHANCEMENT

Speculation about how a person comes to describe his or her unique self, and
how that self is viewed has given rise to several theories on self-concept development (Gergen 1971; Wylie 1978; Rosenberg 1979). The most prevailing of these
theories have their base in those life-propelling forces—human needs, motivation,
and reinforcement—forces which also predominate in the classroom environment.

Need Theories

Both Abraham Maslow (1954, 1968) and William Schutz (1958, 1966)
have developed theories of motivation based on need fulfillment. Maslow's hierarchy of needs has seven levels: physiological needs (suitable air, water and food),
safety needs (protection against physical harm or danger), belongingness-love
needs (affiliation and affection), esteem needs (self-respect and respect of others),
self-actualization needs (the development of one's unique potential), knowledge

and understanding needs (the need to order the unknown), and aesthetic needs (the need for beauty and betterment of self and the environment). Maslow contends that the lower needs must be satisfied before one's attention moves to higher needs. It is interesting to note that in times of crisis and disaster (for example, a tornado), the focus returns to basic needs. It is not likely for a tornado victim to be concerned with the development of self-actualization during such a crisis. The social commentary novelist Tom Wolfe has called the seventies the "me" decade—a time of increased personal introspection with a flurry of sensitivity groups and training in self-improvement. Why? Maslow would contend that it is a time in which many Americans have experienced more economic and political security than ever before, and so the basic needs are satisfied. Thus, attention to self-improvement, at times bordering on egocentric selfishness, is possible. What does this hierarchical fulfillment of needs suggest for the development of self-concept and for the role of the teacher in this development?

First, the very act of satisfying needs, the manner in which an individual satisfies his or her needs, and how effectively this is done all contribute to the sense of self, the self-image. Is the person successful in meeting his or her needs? To what degree, and how easily is that success achieved? And, as the person moves beyond the physiological and safety needs and looks toward satisfying relationships with others and defining self as a unique individual—how is that done? How easily? How successfully?

Second, a student who is tired, hungry, or in need of reassurance of physical safety will not have the energy and resources to devote to the knowledge and understanding needs expected by the teacher. Classroom environments which are unpredictable and threatening will detract from the student's motivation for learning—there are too many lower level needs (perhaps caused by distractions) for the student to satisfy. The teacher can assist by reducing these distractions wherever possible (for example, presenting organized materials, responding to student signs of restlessness and needs for physical movement, and ensuring a safe learning environment).

Outcomes which, following Maslow's theory, discourage a student's attention to classroom performance are also predicted by Schutz's theory of interpersonal needs. Briefly, Schutz emphasizes that *human interaction is a basic need—we need to communicate with others.* This interaction is evident in several ways. A person has the need to *express* affection, inclusion of others, and control, and also has the need to *seek* affection, inclusion, and control from others. Research correlating these interpersonal needs of affection, inclusion, and control with self-concept indicates that individuals with high self-concepts are more open to others (affection), demonstrate more leadership behaviors (control), and are more involved with more people (inclusion) (Thompson 1972). Neglecting this need for human interaction—a need that extends from the social environment of the family into the classroom learning environment—is likely to impede the demands for teacher excellence in classroom performance.

Another consideration in this discussion of needs and classroom behavior is the *needs of the teacher*. How does the teacher perceive himself or herself? How does the teacher satisfy his or her *own* needs for safety, belongingness, esteem, and actualization? What happens when the teacher's needs are not met? Are the needs of the teacher and the student(s) compatible? For example, at a given point in time, do the teacher and students have similar needs for progress, for resolution of classroom upsets and confusions, for reassurance of personal worth? Does the student's need for assistance match the teacher's need to help? How close is the fit? What systems of instruction can be developed which maximize both teacher and student needs, and advance the academic concerns and demands placed on both teachers and students?

Rosenberg (1979) identified two needs (motivational forces) which influence school achievement: the need to think well of self (the self-esteem motive), and the need to maintain self as viewed by self (the self-consistency motive.) Findings on the relationship between self-esteem and school grades indicate a stable and positive relationship, one which seems to perpetuate itself—students who do well in school report high levels of self-esteem, and students with high self-esteem are predicted accurately to be high achievers. However, it is also the case that students who do not think well of themselves may have a need for self-consistency which is so strong that they will protect an "average" self-image by maintaining average grades even when excellence is possible. In various contexts, this response has been called the "fear of success phenomenon." Such behavior indicates the strength of the need to maintain self-consistency, to maintain and even *prove* the image one holds for self as true. Support of this self-consistency motive is illustrated clearly in a variety of studies reported by Braun (1976) in which the student purposefully achieves less or reports more dissatisfaction with self when the grade received surpasses the self-expectation. In a typical study, students who expect to do poorly and receive confirming evidence to this effect report more satisfaction with themselves than do students who expect to do poorly and are told they did much better than expected! One of the most difficult tasks for a teacher is to break this protective casing of a student's confirmed self-image. The student expects negative criticism, accepts it as a part of self, resists information to the contrary, and may even behave so as to elicit such criticism. The self-consistency motive is strong and quite difficult to counteract.

Reflected Appraisal Theory

The role of the teacher in shaping a student's self-concept is also powerful. The teacher's influence extends beyond the theories of personal and interpersonal needs to a process known as "reflected appraisal." Reflected appraisal refers to the theory that a person's ideas about self are affected by what that person thinks *others* think of him or her (Cooley 1902; Mead 1934; Gergen 1971; Rosenberg 1979). The "others" included in these appraisals are those individuals who are important to the person, those who matter, who make a difference to the person. They are *significant others*—the persons sought out for guidance and direction. Who are significant others? Research studies have indicated that without regard to sex, race, age, or socioeconomic status, the order of significant others is quite stable: mother, father, siblings, teachers, friends, classmates (Rosenberg 1979). With such a predictable ranking, consider the effect a teacher can have with his or her students. Depending on grade level, students spend thirty to fifty hours a week (of "prime time" energy) in a classroom—an environment from which all of the higher-ranked significant others are absent. How the teacher views the students is central to their perception of self, which in turn can affect their academic performance.

In a study of Mexican-American and Anglo ninth graders, Carter (1968) found little difference in how the two ethnic groups rated themselves on self-esteem. However, the teachers and administrators were convinced that the Mexican-American students had lower self-esteem, and offered a number of persuasive arguments to support their erroneous conclusions. Putting this attitudinal variable into an equation for teacher expectancy effects, one can predict less than positive results for the Mexican-American students.

Social Comparison Theory

Along with the influence of the teacher on student self-concept, other individuals in the classroom—the classmates—have an effect. Analysis of these student-student interactions is the focus of research studies in *social comparisons.* Pettigrew (1967) has identified two criteria used to develop a self-view. The student looks at self first in relation to others in the environment, and second in relation to certain defined standards, for example, grading criteria, and the teacher's specific task descriptions and rules. For social comparisons among students, research indicates that students use other students in their *immediate environment* as comparison points and not all of American society, as is more common with adult comparisons. For example, a common misconclusion of social comparison theory is that Black children have lower levels of self-esteem than Anglo children. Studies reported by Rosenberg and Simmons (1973) indicated no significant difference in self-esteem levels for the two groups of children. They account for this by noting that the groups observed interacted in their own ethnic and socioeconomic groups, thus stressing the importance of checking exactly who comprises the comparison groups, and of determining the individual's personal identity with and assignment of importance to the group used in the comparison. If specific information for the comparison groups is not provided, global statements about the relationship between race and self-esteem may be misleading.

Individual Selectivity

For both the reflected appraisal and the social comparison theories of self-concept development, there is an intervening "cog" yet to be considered—that of *individual selectivity*. For both the appraisal and comparison processes, the individual maintains some degree of control over the people identified as significant others and, although less so, as comparison groups. The most obvious example of selectivity involves those people identified as "friends"—we choose our friends. Parents, brothers and sisters are "givens." There is no choice in the matter of family. Teachers for the most part are also givens, as are the other students in class. Yet within this circle of predetermined relationships, one can choose to have more frequent interactions with certain teachers and students than with others. Based on past research findings, predictions can be made about the individuals students choose for more personal interactions—they are individuals who commonly hold views of the student which agree with the student's own view of self. Another selective process operating in the classroom is that of selective credibility. Certain individuals are chosen and perceived by the student as being more valued and credible than others. Other than the complaints that teachers are phony and do not listen to students (Gordon 1974), there are few specific guides as to what makes a credible and valued teacher. Research in interpersonal relationships suggests that factors of perceived attraction, similarity, and power are influential in this determination. Thus, for all the predictions which can be made based on the theories of reflected appraisals and social comparisons, the notion of individual selectivity remains a major filtering consideration.

Interpersonal Perception Method

Because it coordinates many of the principles discussed in the theories presented earlier, the Interpersonal Perception Method (IPM) developed by Laing, Phillipson, and Lee (1966) is one of the most comprehensive systems for viewing self-perception and interpersonal communication. According to this theory, the basic elements to be studied in any dyad is the *self* of each of the members of the dyad. The interaction between the two members is a function of the way in which they (1) perceive themselves, (2) perceive the other person, and (3) see the other person perceiving them. These perceptions, of course, are a function of past experiences with other people, and they affect the way the individuals act and react in novel situations.

In developing a method to determine the shared accuracy of perceptions between members of a dyad—the goal of which is an "ideal match," or balanced state in which perceptions are congruent—Laing asked married couples to indicate three levels of perceptions with respect to six topic areas: (1) interdependence and autonomy, (2) warmth, concern, and support, (3) disparagement and disappointment, (4) contentions: fight versus flight, (5) contradictions and confusion, and (6) extreme denial of autonomy. Because the application of these concepts to the teacher-student relationship should be readily evident, this dyadic relationship (teacher-student) will be used to present the details of this theory.

According to Laing, the three levels of perception used for comparisons are:

1. Direct Perspective (DP): for example, the teacher's perception of student behavior.
2. Metaperspective (MP): for example, the teacher's perception of the student's perception of student behavior.
3. Meta-metaperspective (MMP): for example, the teacher's perception of the student's perception of the teacher's perception of student behavior.

The degree of overlap or matching of these perspectives is crucial for an effective dyadic interaction. Comparisons of the perspectives of the dyad result in eight possible interpersonal effects, as follows:

1. Agreement: Matching of the direct perspective of persons 1 and 2; that is, $DP_1 = DP_2$
2. Disagreement: Mismatching of the direct perspectives of persons 1 and 2; that is, $DP_1 \neq DP_2$
3. Understanding: Matching of one person's direct perspective with the other person's metaperspective; that is, $DP_1 = MP_2$ or $DP_2 = MP_1$
4. Misunderstanding: Mismatching of one person's direct perspective with the other person's metaperspective; that is, $DP_1 \neq MP_2$ or $DP_2 \neq MP_1$
5. Feeling Understood: Matching of one person's direct perspective with his or her own meta-metaperspective; that is, $DP_1 = MMP_1$ or $DP_2 = MMP_2$
6. Feeling Misunderstood: Mismatching of one person's direct perspective with his or her own meta-metaperspective; that is, $DP_1 \neq MMP_1$ or $DP_2 \neq MMP_2$
7. Realization: Matching of one person's metaperspective with the other person's meta-metaperspective; that is, $MP_1 = MMP_2$ or $MP_2 = MMP_1$
8. Lack of Realization: Mismatching of one person's metaperspective with the other person's meta-metaperspective; that is, $MP_1 \neq MMP_2$ or $MP_2 \neq MMP_1$

Using a teacher-student situation, table 8-1 illustrates the possibilities for the results indicating agreement, understanding, feeling understood, and realization.

TABLE 8-1

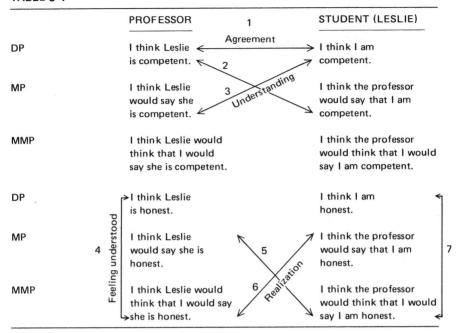

	PROFESSOR	STUDENT (LESLIE)
DP	I think Leslie is competent.	I think I am competent.
MP	I think Leslie would say she is competent.	I think the professor would say that I am competent.
MMP	I think Leslie would think that I would say she is competent.	I think the professor would think that I would say I am competent.
DP	I think Leslie is honest.	I think I am honest.
MP	I think Leslie would say she is honest.	I think the professor would say that I am honest.
MMP	I think Leslie would think that I would say she is honest.	I think the professor would think that I would say I am honest.

(1 Agreement; 2, 3 Understanding; 4 Feeling understood; 5, 6 Realization; 7)

When these comparisons are not congruent, the results are disagreement (for example, Professor: I think Leslie is competent; Student: I don't think I am competent), misunderstanding, feeling misunderstood, and lack of realization.

By analyzing the relationships among the different levels of perspectives, Laing derived a model called the "spiral of perspectives." After analysis of mismatched perspectives, effective strategies may then be developed for coping with any problems identified in the relationship.

In a recent study of teacher-student perceptions, Rosenfeld, Otero, and Civikly (1979) assessed the degree to which college professors and students shared similar perceptions of the student's academic and social behaviors. Professors and students completed questionnaires adapted to Laing's IPM (after Davis 1964) which measured each respondent's direct perspective, metaperspective, and meta-metaperspective concerning academic and social dimensions of the student's behavior. Sample items from the questionnaires are presented in table 8-2. For each item, part A measures the direct perspective, B the metaperspective, and C the meta-metaperspective. Following Laing's system for analyzing the perspectives, it was found that teacher-student perceptual congruency about student social and academic performance was generally high. However, in correlating the perceptions about sharing a good teacher-student relationship

TABLE 8-2 Professor Questionnaire: Sample Items

Cognitive Dimension

A. I think the student has high academic performance.

1	2	3	4	5	6	7
(very false)						(very true)

B. The student would respond that he or she has high academic performance.

1	2	3	4	5	6	7
(very false)						(very true)

C. The student would think that I have responded that he or she has high academic performance.

1	2	3	4	5	6	7
(very false)						(very true)

Social Dimension

A. I think the student is fairminded.

1	2	3	4	5	6	7
(very false)						(very true)

B. The student would say that he or she is fairminded.

1	2	3	4	5	6	7
(very false)						(very true)

C. The student would think that I have responded that he or she is fairminded.

1	2	3	4	5	6	7
(very false)						(very true)

with the perceptions of student behavior, it was found that the more teachers and students agreed about their relationship, the less accurate were their perceptions of the student's behavior. Mutual perceptions of an overall good relationship appear to have been related to overestimations and underestimations of teacher and student perceptions of student behaviors in the classroom. These results, while somewhat surprising, accounted for only 15% of the variance of the correlation, and remained overshadowed by the high degree of teacher–student perceptual congruency. A secondary finding was also of interest—students' sociability, thought to be of minor importance at the university level, was perceived as accurately by professors and students as was the student's academic performance.

From this relatively brief review of theories of self-concept development and enhancement, the role of the teacher as a central figure for the student should be clear. Each approach to self-concept enhancement suggests certain teacher behaviors: the teacher should strive to create a comfortable learning environment, to provide opportunities for personal interaction, to check periodically on the perceptual accuracy shared with the student, and to become a significant other for each student. Assuredly, the achievement of these behaviors is an enormous and difficult task, yet one well worth doing.

TABLE 8-2 (continued)   Student Questionnaire: Sample Items

Cognitive Dimension

A. I think that I have high academic performance.

1	2	3	4	5	6	7
(very false)						(very true)

B. The professor would respond that I have high academic performance.

1	2	3	4	5	6	7
(very false)						(very true)

C. The professor would think that I have responded that I have high academic performance.

1	2	3	4	5	6	7
(very false)						(very true)

Social Dimension

A. I think I am fairminded.

1	2	3	4	5	6	7
(very false)						(very true)

B. The professor would respond that I am fairminded.

1	2	3	4	5	6	7
(very false)						(very true)

C. The professor would think that I have responded that I am fairminded.

1	2	3	4	5	6	7
(very false)						(very true)

ROLE OF THE TEACHER

Whether or not a student does well in school is a function of many variables which researchers asking the question What is an effective teacher? continue to explore (Travers 1973). The role of the student's self-concept and self-esteem are two factors which cannot be overlooked in seeking answers to this question.

Behaviors Characteristic of High Self-Esteem Students

Global findings about behavioral indicators of self-concept development suggest that the following behaviors correlate positively with high self-esteem: The student (1) is unafraid of a new situation, (2) makes friends easily, (3) experiments easily with new materials, (4) trusts the teacher even when a stranger, (5) is cooperative and usually follows reasonable rules, (6) is largely responsible for controlling his or her own behaviors, (7) is creative and imaginative, (8) talks freely and may have had difficulty listening to others due to this eagerness to share own personal experiences, (9) is independent and needs only a minimum amount of direction from the teacher, and (10) seems for the most part to be a happy individual (Survant 1972). Added to these observations are (11) low occurrences of delinquent or disruptive behaviors, (12) the development of effective coping strategies for stress situations, and (13) low levels of communication apprehension (McCroskey 1977).

These behaviors also serve as supportive conditions for the continued enhancement of self-esteem, and it becomes difficult to determine if self-esteem can be identified as the cause or effect of academic achievement. Many of the studies investigating this relationship occur in the midstream of school years, and cannot assess an exact cause-effect relationship. However, the assumption of self-concept as an important intervening variable for achievement is quite strong (Rubin, Dorle, & Sandidge 1977; Scheirer & Kraut 1979).

In an investigation by Wattenburg and Clifford (1964), the relationship between self-esteem and achievement was clarified, suggesting that levels of self-esteem can induce differences in school performance. In this study, kindergarten children were given intelligence and self-esteem tests prior to learning how to read. After two and a half years, it was found that the self-esteem levels were better predictors of the child's reading achievement than was the child's score on the intelligence test.

There are other specific behaviors which have been identified as characteristic of high and low self-esteem students. Students with high self-esteem are characteristically confident in their communication skills and social interactions, talk less about themselves, have an optimistic attitude toward competition, and express and respond to compliments and criticisms in a graceful, accepting manner (Purkey 1970; Coopersmith & Feldman 1974).

Behaviors Characteristic of
Low Self-Esteem Students

Students with low self-esteem characteristically use stereotyped clichés and verbal expressions, are pessimistic about competitive situations, and have difficulty in giving and accepting praise or criticism (Purkey 1970; Coopersmith & Feldman 1974). These students are experts in the art of the self put-down, a self-destructive behavior which Sidney Simon (1977) illustrates in his allegory called *Vulture*. Cues to the teacher that a student might have a low self-image are such statements as the following:

—"I've never been able to do this." (self put-down statement)
—"What's the use, I don't stand a chance." (negative expectations about competition and perseverance)
—"He's really stupid. He was just lucky this time." (criticism of others' achievements)
—"It's not my fault." (unwillingness to accept responsibility)
—"Her problem is that she ——s too much." (readiness to point out faults and failures of others)
—"Oh, you're just saying that to be nice." (inability to accept praise)

The occurrence of such "vulture" statements and other nonverbal indicators of low self-esteem is not uncommon or infrequent. What might the teacher do to lessen such student behaviors and feelings? How can the teacher's attempts in this direction be incorporated and blended with the content material which also demands attention? Coopersmith and Feldman (1974) suggest the following balance of performance orientations and person orientations by the teacher:

> . . . When the question is phrased in terms of a choice, or a statement of priorities between achievement *or* self-esteem, the tendency is to see greater differences between these two goals rather than to recognize that self-esteem is part of performance itself. By fostering positive self-concepts and self-esteem in students, the teacher at the same time promotes academic achievement; by providing certain types of academic experiences, the teacher at the same time fosters positive self-concepts and self-esteem. Thus the resolution is not a choice of *which* to emphasize, but a question of how to develop procedures that increase skills and at the same time promote development of a positive self-concept and self-esteem. (p. 195)

Classroom Conditions to Enhance Positive Self-Concept

Based on the discussion of theories about the development of positive self-concept (Gerben 1971; Rosenberg 1979), there are at least six conditions for the teacher to address.

1. The teacher must be perceived *by the student* as a "significant other."
2. The teacher must be perceived by the student as a credible appraiser and evaluator.
3. The teacher must be consistent in evaluations of the student.
4. The teacher must be accurate in evaluations and not exaggerate opinions of the student. Compliments must be genuine and traceable to behaviors actually accomplished by the student.
5. The teacher must be perceived by the student as personally concerned with the student's development and interests.
6. The student must believe that he or she is responsible for personal achievements.

Regarding the last suggestion, there is a good explanation why no relationship exists between self-esteem and race or between self-esteem and socioeconomic status (SES) for the preadolescent. It is that the student sees race and SES as *assigned* features, and not as aspects of personal accomplishment. As an adult, the relationship between self-esteem and SES is defined, because the adult attributes his or her achievements as the attainment of a "respectable" SES— it is most definitely a personal accomplishment, and therefore reflects on estimates of self-esteem.

Reviewing the six factors described, each is in actuality both a condition and a goal for effective classroom interaction. Suggestions for developing an instructional atmosphere having these characteristics have stressed two concerns: the *attitudinal* requirements of the teacher (Purkey 1970), and the *behavioral* manifestations of these feelings (Coopersmith & Feldman 1974).

Teacher Behaviors
and Instructional Programs

In his book, *Self Concept and School Achievement,* W. W. Purkey (1970) poses a series of questions for teachers who are seeking to help students gain positive, realistic images of themselves. He notes that "in order to influence students, it is necessary to become a significant other in their lives. . . . The way the teacher becomes significant seems to rest on two forces: (1) what he believes, and (2) what he does" (p. 45).

Beliefs held by the teacher are also twofold: beliefs about self, and beliefs (and subsequent expectations) about the students. Angelo Boy and Gerald Pine (1971) have detailed the teacher's beliefs about self in their book *Expanding the Self: Personal Growth for Teachers.* Their premise is that before the teacher can assist students in their self-development, he or she must become an "expanded person." Characteristics of the expanded person include the following: thinks well of self, thinks well of others, sees self in the process of becoming and changing, sees the value of mistakes, is open to new experiences and suggestions, is responsive and spontaneous, and is *not* perfect—but does cope with the problems and difficulties which arise. As a teacher, the expanded person demonstrates respect for the students, for their uniqueness and complexity and capacity. The expanded person as teacher is empathic, has developed the skill of active listening (Gordon 1974), can allow the students to *be* what they are, and can allow them to *become,* to change. The expanded person-teacher also demonstrates unconditional positive regard for each student (Rogers 1961).

The teacher's beliefs about self and about the students become evident in his or her classroom communication and behavior. Some of the questions which teachers might pose to themselves are the following:

1. Do I convey my expectations and confidence that the students can accomplish work, can learn, and are competent?
2. Do I provide well-defined standards of values, demands for competence, and guidance toward solutions to problems?
3. Do I take every opportunity to establish a high degree of private or semiprivate communication with my students?

In the development of a supportive classroom climate, Purkey (1970) identifies six necessary factors: (1) challenge, (2) freedom, (3) respect, (4) warmth, (5) control, and (6) success. Questions which teachers can pose to themselves to judge their effectiveness in each of these areas, and a summary of each area, are presented in table 8–3.

TABLE 8-3 Conditions for a Supportive Classroom Climate

CLASSROOM FACTOR	SUMMARY	QUESTIONS TO POSE TO SELF
Challenge	"A good way to create challenge is to wait until the chances of success are good, and then say; 'This is hard work, but I think that you can do it.'"	—Do I provide challenging problems to the students and encourage their effort at solving the problem? —Do I encourage creative alternative solutions to problems and questions?
Freedom	"What freedom means to the teacher is that students will learn, provided the material appears to be relevant to their lives and provided they have the freedom to explore and to discover its meaning for themselves."	—Do I encourage students to try something new and to join in new activities? —Do I allow students to have a voice in planning and do I permit them to help make the rules they follow?
Respect	"The rule seems to be that whenever we treat a student with respect, we add to his self-respect, and whenever we embarrass or humiliate him, we are likely to build disrespect in him both for himself and for others."	—Do I have genuine respect for the student and for the student's contribution to the class? —Do I communicate this respect to the students and demonstrate this respect in classroom discussions and one-to-one interactions with each student?
Warmth	"A warm and supportive educational atmosphere is one in which each student is made to feel that he belongs in school and that teachers care about what happens to him. It is one in which praise is used in preference to punishment, courtesy in preference to sarcasm, and consultation in preference to dictation."	—Do I spread my attention around and include each student, keeping special watch for the student who may need extra attention? —Do I notice and comment favorably on the things that are important to students? —Do I practice courtesy with my students?
Control	"Classroom control does not require ridicule and embarrassment. The secret seems to be in the leadership qualities of the teacher. When he (she) is prepared for class, keeps on top of the work and avoids the appearance of confusion, explains why some things must be done, and strives for consistency, politeness and firmness, then classroom control is likely to be maintained."	—Do I remember to see small disciplinary problems as understandable, and not as personal insults? —Do I have, and do my students have, a clear idea of what is not acceptable in my class?

TABLE 8-3 (continued)

CLASSROOM FACTOR	SUMMARY	QUESTIONS TO POSE TO SELF
Success	"Perhaps the single most important step that teachers can take in the classroom is to provide an educational atmosphere of success rather than failure."	—Do I permit my students some opportunity to make mistakes without penalty? —Do I set tasks which are, and which appear to the student to be, within his or her abilities? —Do I provide honest experiences of success for my students?

(after Purkey 1970)

Other behaviors applicable to classroom interactions stem from the research on perceptions of an effective communicator (Feingold 1976), which has isolated five basic principles and twenty-five subprinciples for satisfactory interactions. Viewing classroom communication as an interpersonal event, these principles suggest a number of ways in which teachers might facilitate classroom communication. Consideration of each principle and several of the subprinciples for teacher-student interactions illustrates the importance of *being perceived* in a particular way, and stimulates questions for the training of teachers as effective communicators.

1. The effective communicator is perceived as being adept at creating messages.
   a. Messages are perceived as revealing something personal about the communicator.
   b. Messages are perceived as demonstrating that the communicator knows what he or she is talking about.
2. The effective communicator is perceived as being similar in many ways to the receiver.
   a. Messages are perceived as coming from someone who has interests and attitudes which are similar to those of the receiver.
   b. Messages are perceived as coming from someone who is liked by the receiver and others.
3. The effective communicator is perceived as able to appropriately adapt his or her communication to changing situations.
   a. Messages are perceived as coming from someone who is aware of the impact of his or her messages.
   b. Messages are perceived as coming from someone who uses language appropriate to his or her receiver.
   c. Messages are perceived as being responsive to others.
4. The effective communicator is perceived as committed to others.
   a. Messages are perceived as coming from someone who demonstrates concern that the interaction be mutually profitable.
   b. Messages are perceived as coming from someone who demonstrates reliability.

5. The effective communicator is perceived as adept at receiving messages.
   a. Messages are perceived as coming from someone who is sensitive to verbal and nonverbal cues.
   b. Messages are perceived as coming from someone who is interested in hearing what others have to say. (Feingold 1976)

"One of the major ideas underlying programs designed to build self-concepts and self-esteem in the classroom is that the child should become his own source of reward and motivation" (Coopersmith & Feldman 1974, p. 205). The instructional programs developed by Felker (1974) and by Coopersmith and Feldman (1974) share in this goal, although their suggestions for achieving it differ.

Holding a view similar to that popularized by Simon's (1977) "vultures," Felker describes an action program to teach children how to serve as their own reinforcers. The program emphasizes the development of communication skills, both verbal and nonverbal, and includes five recommendations.

1. Adults (teachers) need to praise themselves in front of others. They should serve as models to the child that self-praise is acceptable.
2. Adults (teachers) should guide the child to practical realistic self-evaluations. Students should be able to identify the specific accomplishments for which they deserve recognition.
3. Adults (teachers) should assist the student in setting reasonable goals.
4. Adults (teachers) should provide communication strategy models and specific verbal expressions which the child/student can use to praise self and others.
5. Adults (teachers) should encourage students in class to praise and compliment each other.

Also concerned with the end-goal of student self-direction, Coopersmith and Feldman (1974) have outlined a program for teachers which they call the "encouragement process." There are three major teacher activities involved in this process: fostering a positive outlook, indicating realistic avenues for success, and investing the child with responsibility for his or her own development. In the first stage, fostering a positive outlook, the teacher works to help the student break a pattern of inactivity. This stage involves teacher behaviors which demonstrate to the students that they are accepted and respected whether they succeed or fail. The purpose of this unconditional acceptance is to allow the student to focus fully on the task without fear of personal failure. Two other teacher behaviors which facilitate this first stage are emphasizing the student's strengths rather than weaknesses, and preparing the student for likely difficulties in accomplishing the decided task. The overall intent of this stage then is to develop the student's trust and confidence in self. In a recent study of teacher expectations and student performance, Harris Cooper (1979) noted differences in teacher feedback for high-expectation students and low-expectation students. The distinction is basically this: High-expectation students receive feedback on their effort expenditure, whereas low-expectation students receive feedback about their interactions with the teacher (content, time and duration). Cooper suggests that teachers may in fact be giving high-expectation students encouragement and practice in the learning of *perseverance* and the value of personal effort, while low-expectation students (not having this encouragement) may be less persistent and experience more failure. Accordingly, the low-expectation students may conclude that effort will not influence the outcomes of their performance.

> If arguments to this point are correct, such a perception on the part of low-expectation students may be an accurate reflection of their classroom environment. High-expectation students may be criticized when the teacher perceives them as not having tried and may be praised when efforts are strong. Low-expectation students, however, may be praised and criticized more often for reasons independent of their personal efforts, namely the teacher's desire to control interaction contexts. Greater use of feedback by teachers to control interactions may lead to less belief on the part of students that personal effort can bring about success. (p. 401)

The second stage of the encouragement process asks the teacher to indicate realistic avenues for student success. The teacher should remind the student of his or her knowledge, ability, and past accomplishments. Using past behaviors as a base, the teacher and student then consider alternatives for expanding the student's performance. The identification of goals and of small graduated steps in reaching those goals increases the probability of accomplishment and continuation to other goals.

The third stage of the encouragement process is the most important and often the most difficult—investing the student with responsibility for his or her own growth. The difficulty lies in the teacher's trust that students can take the steps necessary to complete the task, and confidence that the preparation essential to this third step has been achieved. At this stage, teachers may need to assure themselves as much as their students.

The encouragement process described by Coopersmith and Feldman (1974) can be applied to any content area of teaching. In the early years of school, the most basic concerns are reading, writing, communicating, and calculating skills. In later years, even at the college level, the encouragement process may still be necessary, and unfortunately, may even be a new class experience for some students. At any level of instruction, the process can only serve to facilitate the learning at hand, and move the student to a higher challenge. Coopersmith and Feldman offer the following conclusion:

> . . . effective encouragement requires more than simple praise and reassurance. Individualization, graduated steps, recognition of effort, utilizing the

child's interests, and building of specific skills are all part of the teacher's repertoire in helping a child to move onward. Praise, contingent on success and effort exerted voluntarily by the child, and social feedback that helps the child recognize and appreciate his (her) capacities are major conditions that help a child develop an appreciation of his (her) strengths. (pp. 221-22)

SUMMARY

The premise of this chapter has been that facilitation of positive self-concept is an important teacher goal, no matter if the student is male or female, five, nineteen, or fifty-seven years old, rich or poor; no matter if the class is history, spelling or gymnastics. The task of encouraging student self-esteem is a time-consuming one because the teacher must accumulate information about each student's perception of self, and more specifically, how each student views self, how each would like to view self, and how each shows himself or herself to others. In addition, teachers need to take into account certain pressures experienced by students (imposed by self and society)—pressures to think well of self and to have a consistent view of self. The implication of these pressures for student classroom behavior is clear: Students who view self as "average" (or "below average" or "above average") seek to maintain this image in any number of ways, sometimes functional, sometimes dysfunctional.

The role of teachers in countering nonproductive self-images is dependent on one central factor—that they establish themselves as a significant others for students. Given that teachers (aside from family members) are identified by students as significant others, there is a great amount of influence possible, and the effects of a positive student self-concept indicate it is worth the time and effort. In general, students with positive self-concepts demonstrate cooperative and assertive behaviors, and personal responsibility, while those with low self-esteem are more introverted and pessimistic.

Ironically, then, the focus of this chapter on developing positive self-concept in *students* centers on the *teacher's* own self-concept and the role model presented to the students. Does the teacher think well of self? Demonstrate value for self? Communicate respect for self? And, does the teacher acknowledge each student and encourage wherever possible the student's sense of self-respect and self-worth? Is a supportive classroom climate perceived by the students? To what degree does the teacher approximate the characteristics of an effective communicator? The suggestions described earlier for specific teacher behaviors which enhance student self-concept take a variety of forms, yet they have a common goal—student self-direction. It is proposed that teachers can facilitate achieving this goal by (1) developing their own self images, (2) directing their attention to each student's concept of self, and (3) creating a classroom climate of support which encourages positive self-concepts and the benefits which ensue.

SUGGESTED READINGS

BRAUN, C. "Teacher expectation: Sociopsychological dynamics." *Review of Educational Research,* 1976, *46,* 185–213.

This review of research on teacher expectations looks at the theoretical background of expectancy effects and at a number of other related issues: how expectancies are generated in the teacher's mind and communicated to the students, the variables which affect teacher suggestibility and student responses to the cues, and implications for instruction. Braun also provides a model of the cyclical process of classroom expectations.

GERGEN, K. J. *The Concept of Self.* New York: Holt, Rinehart & Winston, 1971.

In less than one hundred pages, Gergen provides a solid review of the study of self, including the development of self-concept, theories about self-concept formation, the presentation of self, and the study of self in interpersonal situations.

GORDON, T. *T.E.T.: Teacher Effectiveness Training.* New York: David McKay Co., Inc., 1974.

Based on the premise that the quality of the teacher-student relationship is most crucial to effective instruction, and that communication skills are the essence of teaching, Gordon presents a system for improving teaching behaviors which also facilitate student and teacher self-concepts. Concepts prominent in Gordon's program include active listening, communication roadblocks, effective verbal and nonverbal messages, and the no-lose method of conflict resolution.

ROSENBERG, M. *Conceiving the Self.* New York: Basic Books, 1979.

In this seminal work, Rosenberg has expanded the concept of *self* to include all of an individual's thoughts and feelings about himself as an object. He meticulously reviews research on the nature of the self-concept, the role of significant others, differences in self-concept for children and adults, and the relationship of groups to self-identity. He also discusses common disturbances to the self-concept and stresses the influence of social structures on the individual's perception of self.

SIMON, S. *Vulture: A Modern Allegory to the Art of Putting Oneself Down.* New York: Argus Communications, 1977.

In this short paperback designed for all ages, Simon introduces the concept of the psychological vulture which waits to strike at the first signs of a weak self-image. Through illustrations and storytelling, Simon demonstrates how realistic self-appraisal and positive attitudes can render the vultures harmless.

THOMPSON, W. *Correlates of the Self-Concept.* Studies on the self-concept rehabilitation, Monograph VI, Dede Wallace Center. Nashville, Tenn.: Counselor Recordings and Tests, 1972.

In this monograph, part of a series on self-concept and rehabilitation, Thompson reviews the studies of the relationship of self-concept with age, race, and economic level. He also reports research correlating self-concept with such traits and behaviors as dogmatism, anxiety, self-disclosure, and interpersonal relationships. The series, based on research from the Tennessee Self-Concept Scale, includes other monographs on self-concept and delinquency, self-actualization, interpersonal competence, psychopathology, and performance.

REFERENCES

BOY, A. V., and G. J. PINE. *Expanding the Self: Personal Growth for Teachers.* Dubuque, Iowa: William C. Brown Co., Publishers, 1971.

BRAUN, C. "Teacher expectation: Sociopsychological dynamics." *Review of Educational Research,* 1976, *46,* 185–213.

CARTER, T. P. "Negative self-concepts of Mexican-American children." *School and Society,* 1968, *96,* 217–19.

COOLEY, C. H. *Human Nature and the Social Order.* New York: Charles Scribner's Sons, 1902.

COOPER, H. M. "Pygmalion grows up: A model for teacher expectation communication and performance influence." *Review of Educational Research,* 1979, *49,* 389–410.

COOPERSMITH, S. and R. FELDMAN. "Fostering a positive self concept and high self-esteem in the classroom." In R. H. Coop and K. White (eds.) *Psychological Concepts in the Classroom.* New York: Harper & Row, 1974.

DAVIS, J. A. *Faculty Perceptions of Students: The Development of the Student Rating Form, Part I.* Princeton, N.J.: Educational Testing Service, 1964.

FEINGOLD, P. C. "Toward a Paradigm of Effective Communication: An Empirical Study of Perceived Communicative Effectiveness." Unpublished Ph.D. Dissertation, Purdue University, 1976.

FELKER, D. W. *Building Positive Self-Concepts.* Minneapolis, Minn.: Burgess Publishing Co., 1974.

GERGEN, K. J. *The Concept of Self.* New York: Holt, Rinehart & Winston, 1971.

GORDON, T. *T.E.T.: Teacher Effectiveness Training.* New York: David McKay Co., Inc., 1974.

LAING, R. D., H. PHILLIPSON, and A. R. LEE. *Interpersonal Perception: A Theory and a Method of Research.* New York: Springer Publishing Co., 1966.

McCROSKEY, J. C. *Quiet Children and The Classroom Teacher.* Annandale, Va.: Speech Communication Association, 1977.

MASLOW, A. H. *Motivation and Personality.* New York: Harper & Row Publishers, Inc., 1966.

MASLOW, A. H. *Toward a Psychology of Being* (2nd ed.). New York: D. Van Nostrand Company, 1968.

MEAD, G. H. *Mind, Self and Society.* Chicago: University of Chicago Press, 1934.

PETTIGREW, T. F. "Social evaluation theory: Convergences and applications." In D. Levine (ed.), *Nebraska Symposium on Motivation.* Lincoln, Nebr.: University of Nebraska Press, 1967, 241–311.

PURKEY, W. W. *Self-Concept and School Achievement.* Englewood Cliffs, N.J.: Prentice-Hall, Inc., 1970.

ROGERS, C.   *On Becoming a Person.* Boston: Houghton Mifflin, 1961.

ROSENBERG, M.   *Conceiving the Self.* New York: Basic Books, 1979.

ROSENBERG, M., and R. G. SIMMONS.   *Black and White Self-Esteem: The Urban School Child.* Washington, D.C.: American Sociological Association, 1973.

ROSENFELD, L. B., M. W. OTERO, and J. M. CIVIKLY.   "Shared interpersonal perceptions of college professors and students." Unpublished paper, Department of Speech Communication, University of New Mexico, 1979.

RUBIN, R. A., J. DORLE, and S. SANDIDGE.   "Self-esteem and school performance." *Psychology in the Schools,* 1977, *14,* 503–6.

SCHEIRER, M. A., and R. E. KRAUT.   "Increasing educational achievement via self-concept change." *Review of Educational Research,* 1979, *49,* 131–50.

SCHUTZ, W.   *FIRO: Fundamental Interpersonal Relations Orientation.* New York: Holt, Rinehart & Winston, 1958.

SCHUTZ, W.   *The Interpersonal Underworld.* Palo Alto, Calif.: Science & Behavior Books, 1966.

SIMON, S.   *Vulture: A Modern Allegory to the Art of Putting Oneself Down.* New York: Argus Communications, 1977.

SURVANT, A.   "Building positive self-concepts." *Instructor,* 1972, *81,* 94–95.

THOMPSON, W.   *Correlates of the Self-Concept.* Studies on the self-concept rehabilitation, Monograph VI, Dede Wallace Center. Nashville, Tenn.: Counselor Recordings and Tests, 1972.

TRAVERS, R. M. W.   *Handbook of Research on Teaching* (2nd ed.). Skokie, Ill.: Rand McNally & Company, 1973.

WATTENBERG, W. W. and C. CLIFFORD.   "Relation of self-concepts to beginning achievement in reading." *Child Development,* 1964, *35,* 461–67.

WYLIE, R. C.   *The Self-Concept; Volume 2: Theory and Research on Selected Topics.* Lincoln, Nebr.: University of Nebraska Press, 1978.

INDEX